Françoise Vauzeilles
Photographs by Julie Robert

MACRAMÉ

25 projects to create with cord

Hardie Grant
BOOKS

INTRODUCTION

Some cord, a pair of scissors and basic knots are all you need to get started with macramé!

Discover a simple technique you can learn in no time and make useful and decorative projects for the home and everyday life by simply following the explanations in this book.

Once you've got to grips with double half hitches, square knots and gathering knots, it's time to take the plunge and give your creativity free rein with these fun and original pieces.

Macramé designs often feature in folk art but can also be elevated to the level of fine art and fit perfectly into both classic and contemporary interiors. Add some gold or copper yarn, colour your cord with vegetable dyes, create new ways of using knots or make them with thick cord – in other words, the key thing here is to have fun!

CONTENTS

EQUIPMENT AND SUPPLIES

You don't need lots of equipment or much in the way of supplies to do macramé. A good sharp pair of scissors is enough to get started with. Some of the more complex projects require a bit more equipment, but nothing expensive or that you won't have in a toolbox or sewing kit.

In terms of supplies, you're going to be using different types of cord. This can be cable cord or braided, and made from leather, cotton, etc., but should always be of good quality so that your projects look beautiful and stand the test of time. Some projects require a lot of cord, so make sure you always have enough to complete them – better to have too much than not enough!

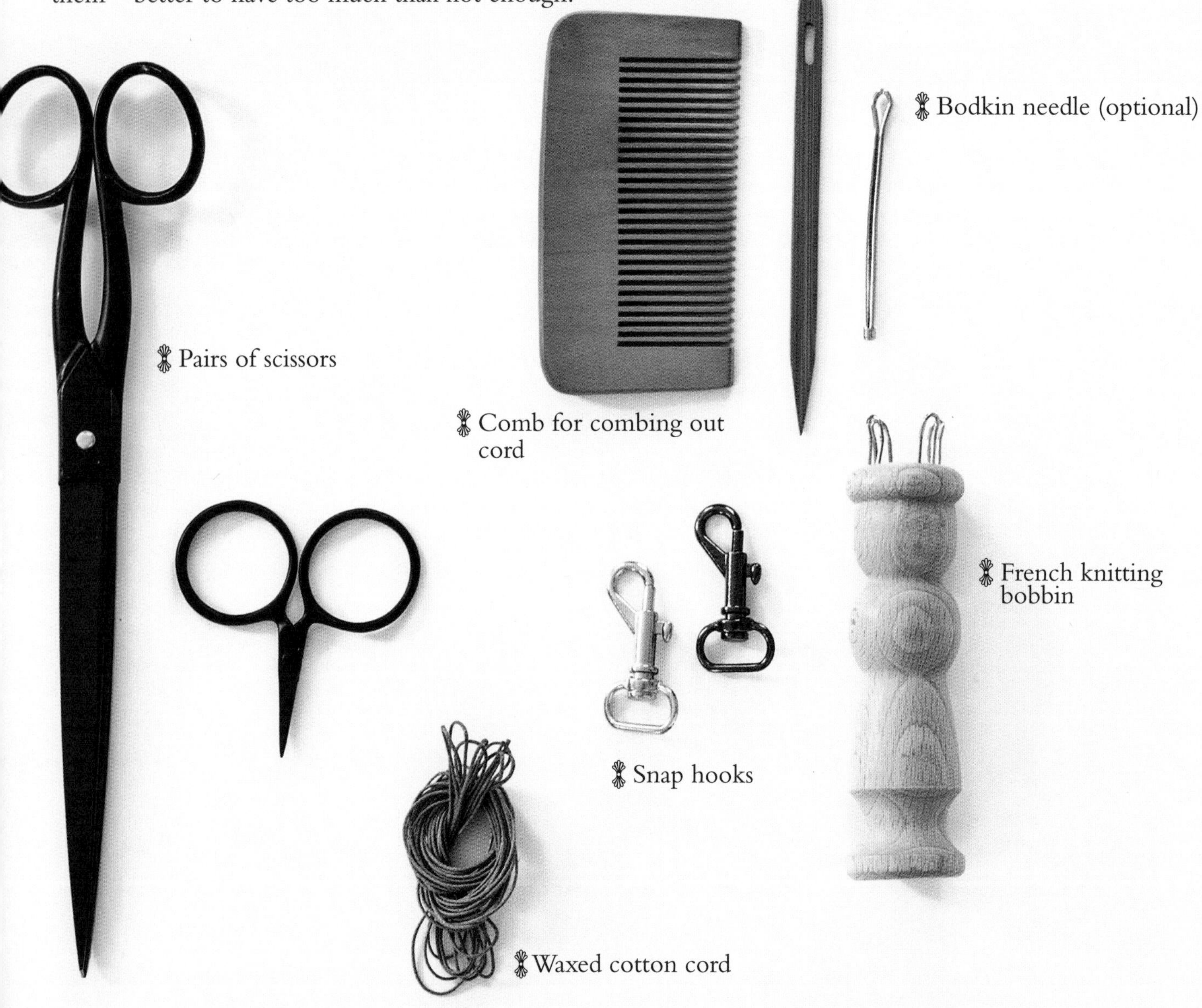

Bodkin needle (optional)

Pairs of scissors

Comb for combing out cord

French knitting bobbin

Snap hooks

Waxed cotton cord

Ruler

Recycled cotton thread

Braided cord

Cable cord
(8 mm/5/16 in)

Cable cord
(4 mm/5/32 in)

Upholstery piping cord

LIKE A PRETZEL

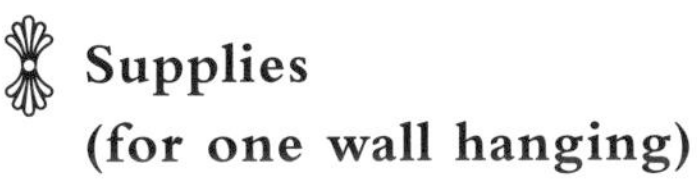

Supplies (for one wall hanging)

330 cm (10¾ ft)of 6 mm (¼ in) piping cord (or cable cord)
1 skein of gold thread

Equipment

1 pair of scissors

Knot used

Josephine knot
(see page 70)

Make a Josephine knot with 3 x 110 cm (3½ ft) lengths of cord, starting 20 cm (8 in) from the top of the cords to centre the knot. Work with one piece of cord on the left and two on the right. Pull on the ends of the pieces of cord to shape the knot, making sure it stays flat.

Added extra

Wrap gold thread in different places around the ends of the cords or at different heights.

ROPE LIGHT

Supplies (for a 4 m [13 ft] rope light)

40 m (131 ft) of 2 mm (3/32 in) braided cord

4 m rope light

Knots used

Overhand knot
(see page 65)

Double overhand knot
(see page 65)

Square knot
(see page 66)

Fold the cord in half. Using an overhand knot, tie the cord halfway along its length to the end of the rope light, at the opposite end from the plug. Tie a succession of square knots around the rope light to cover its whole length. Finish with a double overhand knot.

Good to know

To calculate the amount of cord you'll need, multiply the length of the rope light by 10.

BRAIDED WREATH

Supplies (for one wreath)

10 m (32¾ ft)of 3 mm (⅛ in) cable cord

1 metal hoop, 15 cm (6 in) in diameter

Equipment

1 pair of scissors

Knot used

Overhand knot
(see page 65)

Fold 3 x 330 cm (10¾ ft) lengths of cord in half and place them under the hoop, which will give you 6 cords that you can group into 3 sets of 2 cords.
Tie a 3-strand braid (each strand comprising 2 cords) from left to right, around the metal hoop so that it is hidden by the braid.

When the braid covers the whole hoop, tie an overhand knot with the 6 pieces of cord.You can then cut off the cords or use them to hang the wreath.

Handy hint

As a general rule, to calculate the length of cord you'll need, multiply the circumference of the hoop by 3.5.

Added extra

You can stick foliage, dried flowers or decorative items made from white modelling clay onto the wreath.

MONKEY'S FIST DOORSTOP

Supplies

10 m (32¾ ft) of 1 cm (⅜ in) upholstery piping cord

1 wooden ball, 10 cm (4 in) in diameter

Knot used

Monkey's fist knot
(see page 68)

Hold the wooden ball in one hand and wrap the cord vertically around your fingers and the ball 10 times, tightening the turns of the cord snugly against each other. Then wrap the cord 10 times horizontally around the ball and the vertical turns of cord, tightening the turns of the cord snugly against each other. To finish, wrap the cord 10 times around the ball and the horizontal cords by threading it underneath the first vertical turns so that the wooden ball is completely covered.

Starting with the first turn of the cord, pull on it to tighten each turn of cord around the ball one after the other to create a tight monkey's fist knot. If you want to make a tie handle, form a loop with the cord in the middle of the monkey's fist and then continue tightening the cord to the end.

FRINGED LAMPSHADE

Supplies

77 m (252¾ ft) of 2 mm (3/32 in) cable cord

1 lampshade frame, 20 x 10 x 15 cm (8 x 4 x 6 in)

Equipment

1 pair of scissors

Knots used

Lark's head knot (see page 64)

Overhand knot (see page 65)

Square knot (see page 66)

Alternating square knots (see page 67)

Start by covering the uprights connecting the two hoops of the lampshade frame with cord. For each upright, cut 150 cm (5 ft) of cord and fold it 30 cm (12 in) from one end. Tie it to the upper hoop, to the right of an upright, with a lark's head knot.

Using the longest piece of cord and holding the shortest piece against the upright, tie a succession of overhand knots along the upright until you get to the base: pass the longest piece of cord under the metal part and the shortest piece of cord by forming a loop to the right, then thread it over and through the loop and tighten. When you get to the bottom, tie a knot on either side of the upright: wrap the cord from front to back around the base of the lampshade, thread through the loop and tighten securely. Cover the other uprights of the lampshade in the same way.

Then work on the sections between the uprights.

For each section, fold 6 x 120 cm (4 ft) lengths of cord in half and hang them over the top of the lampshade between two uprights.

Tie 9 rows of alternating square knots spaced about 1.5 cm (½ in) apart, starting with a row of 3 square knots and finishing with 3 square knots in the 9th row.

Row 1: 3 square knots
Row 2: 2 square knots
Row 3: 3 square knots
Row 4: 2 square knots
Row 5: 3 square knots
Row 6: 2 square knots
Row 7: 3 square knots
Row 8: 2 square knots
Row 9: 3 square knots

Then tie an overhand knot as close as possible to the square knots.

To attach your work to the bottom hoop, tie a lark's head knot with 2 x 30 cm (12 in) lengths of cord folded in half, incorporating the rim and bottom of the macramé between square knots. Cut the cords to create fringes.

SIDE TABLE

Supplies

112 m (367½ ft) of 4 mm (5/32 in) cream recycled cotton cord

1 folding camping stool frame

Equipment

1 pair of scissors

Knots used

Overhand knot
(see page 65)

Square knot
(see page 66)

Alternating square knots
(see page 67)

Two rows of vertical double half hitches (see page 73)

Two rows of diagonal double half hitches to form a V shape
(see page 74)

⋆ to ⋆

This abbreviation denotes repeated sections of a pattern. On the rows, the sequences of knots to be repeated are written between the two ⋆ symbols.

Lay 48 x 230 cm (7½ ft) lengths cord vertically and flat one against the other. 60 cm (2 ft) from the top, create 19 rows of alternating square knots, ensuring that they're tied tightly. Once completed, the remaining ends of the cord should be around 60 cm (2 ft) in length.

Then mount the macramé on the stool structure.

Wrap each top cord around the first leg of the stool then tie two rows of vertical double half hitches. Tighten and tie a row of square knots.

⋆Then work in groups of 8 cords: tie a square knot with the 4 central cords. Then make a row of diagonal double half hitches with the 4 left strands and a row of diagonal double half hitches with the 4 right strands to create a point in the middle.

Finish the point with an overhand knot. Repeat the same procedure on the remaining 40 cords. This will create 6 points.

Cut all the fringes to the same length (approximately 10 cm [4 in]).⋆

Repeat the same procedure from ⋆ to ⋆ to attach the bottom of the macramé to the second leg of the stool.

Handy hint

Warning: this small side table cannot support heavy items. As the cord tends to stretch, it's essential to make sure your work is pulled tight. Once you've placed a few magazines and a cup of tea on top of the macramé, it will assume the right shape.

ROUND MIRROR

Supplies

10 m (32¾ ft)of 3 mm (⅛ in) cable cord

36 m (118 ft) of 2 mm (3⁄32 in) cable cord

1 piece of round cork, 18 cm (7 in) in diameter

1 round mirror, 15 cm (6 in) in diameter

1 metal hoop, 18 cm (7 in) in diameter

Equipment

1 pair of scissors

1 bodkin needle

1 tube of glue

Knots used

Overhand knot
(see page 65)

Square knot
(see page 66)

Gathering knot
(see page 70)

Two rows of diagonal double half hitches to form a V shape
(see page 74)

Cut 3 x 330 cm (10¾ ft) lengths of 3 mm (⅛ in) cable cord, fold in half and place them over the hoop, side by side. This gives you 3 groups of 2 cords (the two cords from each group will be used together for the plaiting).

Make a plait around the whole hoop, incorporating it into the plait, then tie an overhand knot with the 6 pieces of cord.

Cut 54 x 60 cm (2 ft) lengths of 2 mm (3⁄32 in) cable cord. Insert them into the plait under every other cord using a bodkin needle, ensuring that the ends are the same length and tie an overhand knot as close as possible to the plait.

Take 3 consecutive groups of 2 cords (both ends of each cord are used double and count as one cord) and tie:
Row 1: 3 square knots
Row 2: 2 square knots
Row 3: 1 square knot

Finish the triangle with two rows of diagonal double half hitches to form a V shape. The ends of the cords used to make the triangle will be combed out to make fringes. Make 8 other triangles in the same way.

Tie a square knot around the 6 ends of the plait cords, using 2 cords from the left triangle and 2 cords from the right triangle then gather these 10 cords together.

Separate the cords into 2 groups of 5. Measure 6 cm (2¼ in) from the square knot and tie a gathering knot 2.5 cm (1 in) long on each group of cords, using 1 m (3¼ ft) of 2 mm (3⁄32 in) cable cord. Then tie a gathering knot 1 cm (⅜ in)long around the 10 cords, using 1 m (3¼ ft) of 2 mm (3⁄32 in) cable cord.

Cut off the fringe cords 3 cm (1¼ in)from the triangles, then comb them out. Glue the mirror and macrame onto the round piece of cork.

GLASSES CORD

Supplies

16 m (52½ ft) of 1 mm waxed cotton cord

2 rubber glasses chain holders

2 metal end caps

Equipment

1 French knitting bobbin

1 pair of small jewellery pliers

1 pair of scissors

Knot used

French knitting

(see page 75)

Use the waxed cotton to make an 85 cm (2¾ ft) cord using a French knitting bobbin and finish with a double knot. Place each knot inside a metal end cap and clamp shut with a pair of jewellery pliers.

DECORATIVE JARS

Supplies

17 m of 2 mm braided cord

1 glass jar

Equipment

1 pair of scissors

Knots used

Lark's head knot
(see page 64)

Double overhand knot
(see page 65)

Alternating square knots
(see page 67)

Two rows of diagonal double half hitches to form a V shape
(see page 74)

Lay an 80 cm (2½ ft) length of cord flat horizontally. Tie 23 x 70 cm lengths of cord to it with lark's head knots created halfway along each cord. Both ends of each cord will be used double and count as one cord.

Wrap the horizontal cord around the opening of the jar and tie a double overhand knot. Do not cut the cord. The ends will be added to the other cords and used to tie knots.

Separate the cords into 3 groups of 8 cords then tie 3 triangles of alternating square knots.

Border each triangle with two rows of diagonal double half hitches to form a V shape. Then make 3 inverted triangles of alternating square knots between the triangles already created.

Cut the ends of the cords so they hang just above the bottom of the jar.

Added extra

Try your hand at dyeing cords by following the instructions on pages 62 and 63.

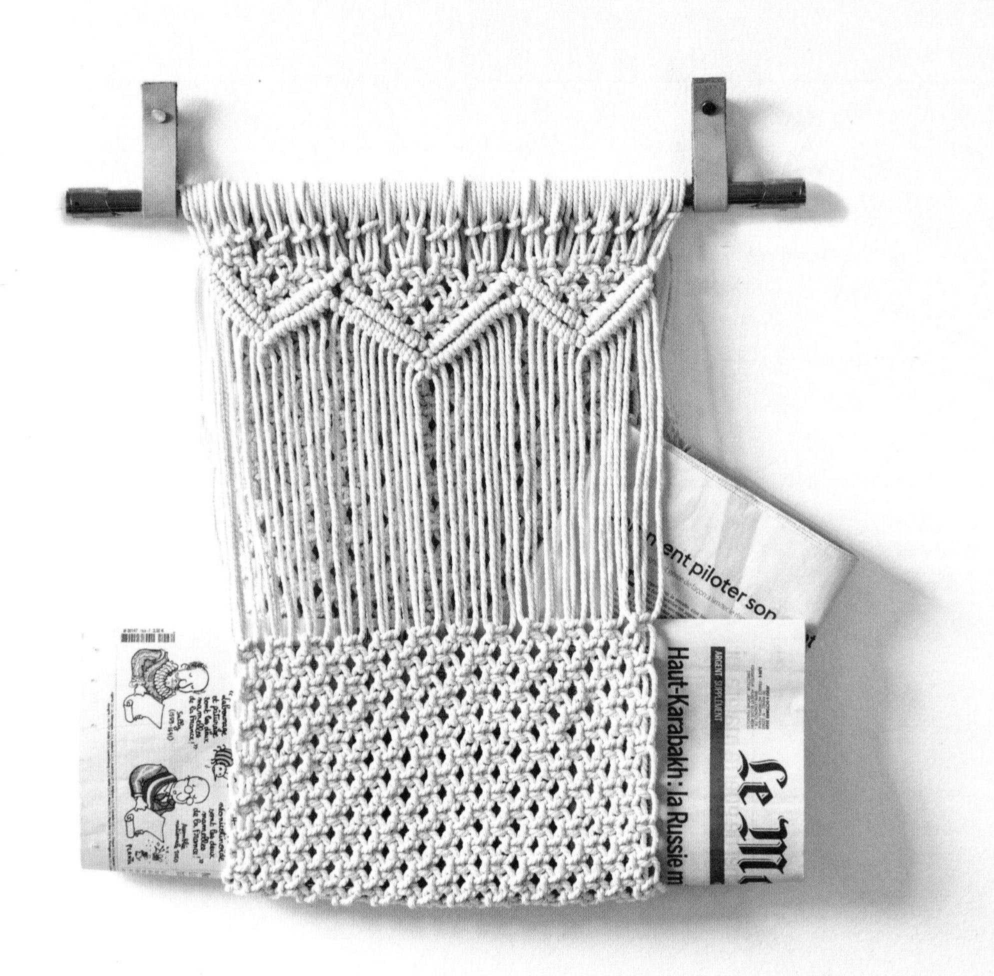
Haut-Karabakh : la Russie

WALL-MOUNTED MAGAZINE RACK

Supplies

120 m of 3 mm cable cord

One 50 cm copper bar 1 cm in diameter

Equipment

1 pair of scissors

Knots used

Square knot
(see page 66)

Two rows of diagonal double half hitches to form a V shape
(see page 74)

Cut 24 x 5 m lengths of cord, fold them in half and tie them to the copper bar with lark's head knots to create cords of the same length. Work in square knots, following the knot layout below:

Row 1: 12 square knots.

Row 2: 4 free cords – 2 square knots – 6 free cords – 3 square knots – 6 free cords – 2 square knots – 4 free cords.

Row 3: 12 free cords – 1 square knot – 22 free cords – 2 square knots – 22 free cords – 2 square knots – 12 free cords.

Row 4: 22 free cords – 1 square knot – 22 free cords.

This will give you a pattern of 3 points, with the central point being slightly larger than the other two.

Frame the three points with 2 rows of diagonal double half hitches to form a V. Repeat. Then, 15 cm below the point of the central triangle, tie 49 rows of alternating square knots. Fold this section in half and backwards to form a pocket. Wrap the 48 cords evenly around the copper bar in between the original 24 lark's head knots. Tighten and finish with a row of square knots.

SIMPLE PLANT HANGER

Fournitures

Supplies

59.5 m of 4 mm cable cord

2 m of 2 mm cable cord

Equipment

1 reel of coloured thread

1 pair of scissors

Knots used

Square knot
(see page 66)

Half square knot spiral
(see page 66)

Gathering knot
(see page 70)

Mark the middle of 8 x 7 m lengths of 4 mm cable cord with a small piece of coloured thread and gather the cords together. Tie a tight 5-turn gathering knot around them, halfway along the cords, using a 150 cm length of 2 mm cable cord, keeping a free end of approximately 10 cm at each end of this cord. Fold this knot in half to form a loop. This gives you 16 4 mm cords. Tie a tight gathering knot of approximately 8 turns at the base of the loop with a 1 m length of 2 mm cord. Cut the ends of the cord flush with the knot.

Divide the 16 cords into 4 groups of 4. With each group of cords, tie 4 square knots, then 8 half square knots to form a spiral, followed by another 4 square knots.

Then, with the 2 right-hand cords from one group and the 2 left-hand cords from the group to the right, tie a series of 4 square knots 5 cm lower down. This gives you 4 new groups of 4 cords.

With the 2 right-hand cords from one group and the 2 left-hand cords from the group to the right, tie 1 square knot 10 cm lower down.

Gather the 16 cords and tie a tight gathering knot of several turns with 1 m of 2 mm cable cord, approximately 7 cm from the last square knot.

Comb out the ends of the 16 cords.

SAILOR KEY RING

Supplies

320 cm of 3 mm cable cord

80 cm of 2 mm braided cord

1 bolt-snap key ring, 15 mm long

Equipment

1 pair of scissors

Knots used

Overhand knot (see page 65)

Square knot (see page 66)

Gathering knot (see page 70)

Cut 2 x 40 cm lengths of cable cord and then another 2 x 120 cm lengths of cable cord.

Lay the cords flat vertically and side by side as follows: one 120 cm length then the two 40 cm lengths and then the other 120 cm length, all aligned at the top.

Tie 2 overhand knots using these 4 cords 8 cm from the top of the cords. Insert the 2 middle cords (40 cm) into the snap hook, then tie 2 overhand knots.

Leave the cords free for 1.5 cm and continue tying square knots until only 8 cm of cord remains. Fold the macramé in half to form a loop and position the two ends of the free cords opposite each other. Tie a gathering knot around the free cords and the original ends of the macramé with an 80 cm length of braided cord. Cut all the cords flush with the knot.

COASTER

Supplies (for a coaster 10 cm in diameter)

16 m of 3 mm cable cord

Equipment

1 pair of scissors

1 support pad (cardboard or cork)

A few pins

Knots used

Lark's head knot (see page 64)

Double overhand knot (see page 65)

Diagonal double half hitch (see page 72)

Fold 5 x 80 cm lengths cord in half and place them flat and vertically next to each other.

Fold a 150 cm length of cord to create one end of 40 cm and another of 110 cm (this will be the knot bearer). Lay this folded cord horizontally on top of the other cords. The loop created at the fold should be to the right of the vertical cords and extend slightly beyond them. Tie the vertical cords to the horizontal one with lark's head knots.

Insert the ends of the horizontal cord into the loop and tighten to form a circle.

Place the work flat on the support pad with the cords radiating out from the centre evenly, and pin the centre to the pad. Hold the long cord (the knot bearer) in your left hand and wrap the first cord to its right around it, bringing it under then over, and between the two cords. Wrap the same cord around the knot bearer in the same way. You've just completed the first knot in a line of diagonal double half hitches.

Keep tying diagonal double half hitches, working in a spiral. To ensure the coaster stays flat, as soon as the gap between two knots looks too large, regularly add a piece of cord by tying it with a lark's head knot and cut it to the same length as the cord to its right.

When the coaster has reached 10 cm in diameter, tie a tight double overhand knot.

Cut the ends of the cords to around 2.5 cm and comb them out.

Handy hint

You can use the same technique to make round place mats.

RAINBOW DECORATION

Supplies

250 cm of 1 cm cable cord

1 ball of yellow gradient cotton thread (50 g = 80 m)

1 ball of gold Lurex

Equipment

1 embroidery needle

1 pair of scissors

1 comb

Knot used

Square knot
(see page 66)

Cut a 38 cm length of cord to make the smallest arc. Wrap the yellow cotton thread and Lurex around it to cover it completely, either in a random pattern or using the photo as inspiration, leaving 7.5 cm of free cord at each end. Form an arc shape with this first piece of cord.

Place the next piece of cord against this arc and cut it so that its ends line up with the ends of the first arc. Wrap yellow thread and Lurex around it, leaving 7.5 cm of free cord at each end.

Repeat this process to make the next three arcs. Sew the arcs together with large stitches using the yellow cotton thread. Comb out the ends of the cords.

To make the hanger, fold 150 cm of yellow thread in half, then fold in half again and cut the bottom loop. Tie square knots for a length of around 10 centimetres. Sew the hanger to the back of the rainbow.

PENNANT BUNTING

Supplies (for a garland 2 m in length with 10 pennants)

42 m of 3 mm cable cord

Equipment

1 pair of scissors

Knots used

Lark's head knot
(see page 64)

Double overhand knot
(see page 65)

Alternating square knots
(see page 67)

Two rows of diagonal double half hitches to form a V shape
(see page 74)

Using a lark's head knot, tie 8 x 50 cm lengths of cord side by side to a 2 m piece of cord, making sure the cords are all the same length. Tie rows of alternating square knots, decreasing by 1 knot on each row to create a triangle. After the last square knot, tie one double overhand knot. Border the triangle with two rows of diagonal double half hitches to form a V shape. Comb out the ends of the cords and cut as required.

Repeat the same process to make the other 9 pennants, spacing them evenly along the 2 mm cord.

STONE LUCKY CHARM

Supplies (for one charm)

7 m of 2 mm cable cord

1 semi-precious stone

Equipment

1 pair of scissors

Knots used

Overhand knot (see page 65)

Alternating square knots (see page 67)

Half hitch chain (see page 70)

Gathering knot (see page 70)

Lay out 5 x 1 m lengths of cord vertically and flat. Align the top of a 150 cm length of cord with the top of the other pieces of cord.

Measure 46 cm from the bottom of the longer cord and tie 20 consecutive tightly spaced half-hitch knots around the shorter 5 pieces of cord. Fold in half to form a loop and use a 30 cm length of cord to tie a 3-turn gathering knot around all the pieces of cord.

Then separate the pieces of cord into 3 groups of 4 cords. Tie 3 rows of 3 alternating square knots, spacing them to match the length of your stone. Place the stone in the centre and complete with an overhand knot tied with the 12 pieces of cord.

Cut them to create a fringe of around 10 centimetres in length.

THE ORGANIC COMPANY®

WATER BOTTLE HOLDER

Supplies

21 m of 2 mm cable cord

One 500 ml water bottle

1 ring-shaped metal snap hook, 15 mm long

Equipment

1 pair of scissors

Knots used

Lark's head knot (see page 64)

Overhand knot (see page 65)

Square knot (see page 66)

Alternating square knots (see page 67)

Gathering knot (see page 70)

Start working from the bottom of the holder upwards. Lay out a 250 cm length of cord horizontally. Attach 7 pieces of cord of the same length using lark's head knots, centring them along the cord and ensuring they're all the same length. Tie in a circle with a tight overhand knot and cut the ends of the cord flush with the knot. This forms the base of the net.

Tie 10 rows of alternating square knots spaced 2 cm apart. Once completed, this gives you 4 groups of 4 cords.

To make the handle, take 2 groups of 4 cords and tie 9 cm of square knots 8 cm from the last row of alternating square knots. Repeat with the other 2 groups of 4 cords.

Gather the 16 cords together, leave a gap of 3 cm and tie 2 square knots with all the cords. Slide the snap hook onto the cords, and tie 2 square knots again with all the cords.

Fold the ends of the cords back to form a loop and tie a tight gathering knot of 10 turns around all the cords with a 1 m length of cord. Cut the ends of the cords flush with the knot.

Handy hint

Match the size of the net to the size of your bottle by spacing the alternating square knots appropriately.

BOTTLE DECORATION

Supplies (for one bottle)

6.5 m of 2 mm cable cord

5 m of 2 mm cable cord (optional, for a tassel)

1 glass bottle

Equipment

1 bodkin needle

1 pair of scissors

Knots used

Gathering knot (see page 70)

Box knot braid (see page 71)

Tie a gathering knot around the bottle to cover around 6 cm.

If you want to add a tassel, cut 16 x 25 cm lengths of cord and gather them into 4 groups of 4 cords. Tie a box knot braid working with 4 double cords, then gather together the ends of the 16 cords. Tie a 3-turn gathering knot around the cords with a 50 cm length of cord.

Pass the remainder of the 50 cm length of cord through the top of the tassel using the bodkin needle, then tie it to one of the loops of cord wrapped around the bottle.

Handy hint

All glass containers can be decorated with natural or dyed cord, regardless of their size or shape. An original way of combining decorative creativity and recycling.

CURTAIN TIEBACK

Supplies (for one tieback)

140 cm of 6 mm cable cord

10 m of 8 mm upholstery piping cord

Equipment

1 pair of scissors

Knots used

Lark's head knot (see page 64)

Overhand knot (see page 65)

Mariner's braid (see page 71)

Gathering knot (see page 70)

Tie an overhand knot at each end of a 70 cm length of cable cord so it doesn't unravel. Lay it horizontally and tie 4 x 250 cm lengths of piping cord to it with lark's head knots, ensuring you have 8 cords of the same length.

Weave a mariner's braid around 75 cm in length, leaving approximately 10 centimetres free at the ends.

Fold the ends of the braid cords in half to form a loop. Tie a tight 3-turn gathering knot at the base of the loop with a 70 cm length of cable cord. Cut the ends of the cord flush with the knot.

Pass one end of the cable cord you started with through the loop, then pass the other end of the cable cord through it in the other direction. Pull on the ends of the cord to tighten.

DOUBLE PLANT HOLDER

Supplies (for one plant holder)

28 m of 3 mm cable cord

1 piece of wood 30 cm in length

Equipment

1 pair of scissors

Knots used

Lark's head knot (see page 64)

Square knot (see page 66)

Alternating square knots (see page 67)

Gathering knot (see page 70)

Tie 9 x 3 m lengths of cord to the piece of wood with lark's head knots to give you 18 identical lengths of cord.

Tie 9 rows of alternating square knots, decreasing by 1 square knot per row on each side, until you have only 1 square knot. This creates a triangle.

Measure 45 cm from the piece of wood and make a symmetrical triangle of the same volume: take 2 cords from the far left side of the vertical cords and 2 cords from the far right side and tie 1 square knot, which will form the tip of the triangle. Then tie 8 rows of alternating square knots, increasing by 1 knot per row on each side by using 2 additional cords to the left and right of the central knot.

When the triangle is completed, bring all the cords together and tie a tight gathering knot of around 10 turns with a 1 m length of cord. Cut the fringes to the length required.

Handy hint

To make a double plant holder, use 56 m of cord and a piece of wood 60 cm in length.

BINOCULARS STRAP

Supplies

45 m of 2 mm cable cord
2 snap hooks

Equipment

1 pair of scissors

Knots used

Square knot
(see page 66)

Double overhand knot
(see page 63)

Gathering knot
(see page 70)

Two rows of diagonal double half hitches to form a V shape
(see page 72)

Cut 16 x 260 cm lengths of cable cord. Identify the midway point of the cords. Align the cords side by side vertically. Start the diamond pattern at the midway point of the cords:

Row 1: tie 1 square knot with the 4 central cords.
Row 2: tie 2 square knots
Row 3: tie 3 square knots
Row 4: tie 4 square knots
Row 5: tie 3 square knots
Row 6: tie 2 square knots

Repeat row 1 to row 6 six times to create 7 diamonds.

Finish with two rows of diagonal double half hitches to form a V shape on each side of the last diamond. This completes half of the strap.

Turn the cords over to make the second half of the strap.

Tie 7 diamonds using square knots as on the first part of the strap and border the last diamond with two rows of diagonal double half hitches to form a V shape.

Tie a gathering knot around the ends of the cords on each side of the strap with 2 lengths of 50 cm cord. Attach a snap hook to each side of the strap using a very tight double overhand knot tied with the ends of 4 cords, as close as possible to the gathering knot. Cut the fringes to the same length on either side of the strap.

Handy hint

This strap can be used in many different ways! Why not adapt it to a camera, beach bag, etc.

FEATHER LEAF

Supplies

10 m of 3 mm cable cord

Equipment

1 pair of scissors

1 comb

Knots used

Reef knot
(see page 65)

Double overhand knot
(see page 65)

Gathering knot
(see page 70)

Fold a 60 cm length of cord in half with the fold positioned at the top. This will form the central rib of the leaf. Tie a 5-turn gathering knot around 3 cm from the top of the rib with a 30 cm length of cord. Tighten the knot and cut the cord flush with it. This creates a loop you can hang the leaf from.

Cut 34 x 25 cm lengths of cord and tie them in pairs along the whole length of the rib using 17 reef knots alternating to the right and left so they sit snugly one against the other. Then tie a double overhand knot with both ends of the rib cord to hold the knots in place and prevent them from slipping.

To finish, comb out the 34 pieces of cord then cut the fringes to create the final shape of the leaf.

Handy hint

You can leave the leaf so that it moves around naturally, or you can stiffen it a little with hairspray or spray starch. You can also use spray adhesive to glue your leaf to a small piece of cardboard cut to its shape.

GLASSFLOAT HANGER

Supplies

22 m of 2 mm cable cord

80 cm of 4 mm cable cord

1 glass ball or float

Equipment

1 pair of scissors

1 small rectangle of cardboard 3.5 cm × 6.5 cm

Knots used

Lark's head knot (see page 64)

Overhand knot (see page 65)

Alternating overhand knot mesh (see page 69)

Gathering knot (see page 70)

Cut 16 x 120 cm lengths of 2 mm cable cord and group them in twos to create 8 groups of 2 cords.

Place a first group of cords horizontally and tie the other groups of cords to it using lark's head knots, ensuring you have identical cord lengths. Tie into a circle with a tight overhand knot.

Tie 5 rows of an alternating overhand knot mesh, spacing each knot 3.5 cm apart. To help you keep this spacing, slide the cardboard rectangle between the cords before tying a knot and tie the cords just above it.

Position the glass ball or float inside the macramé net. Gather the cords together and tie a tight gathering knot of around 10 turns with a 1 m length of 2 mm cable cord. Cut the cords approximately 10 cm from the knot.

Slide the 4 mm cable cord under the circle you made at the beginning of the macramé. Hold the ends together and tie a gathering knot with a 1 m length of 2 mm cable cord which will allow you to hang the float.

MINIMALIST PENDANT LIGHT

Supplies

31 m of 4 mm cable cord

3 m of electric cable

1 light fitting

1 electric plug

1 decorative light bulb

Equipment

1 pair of scissors

1 roll of adhesive tape

Knots used

Square knot (see page 66)

Gathering knot (see page 70)

Fit the light fitting and plug onto the electrical cable.

Cut 30 m of cord and wrap a small piece of tape around each end to stop it from fraying. Identify the midpoint of the cord and tie it to the electric cable using a square knot, as close as possible to the light fitting.

Using a 50 cm length of cord, tie a tight gathering knot of a few turns under the fitting and around the electric cable and original cord, then cut the ends of the 50 cm cord flush with the knot.

Then tie square knots along the entire length of the electrical cable, stopping around 2 cm from the electric plug. To finish, use a 50 cm length of cord to tie a tight gathering knot around the electric cable and original cord. Cut the ends of the cords flush with the knot.

WALL HANGING

Supplies

57.6 m of 2 mm cable cord

14.3 m of 4 mm cable cord

1 embroidery hoop 48 cm in diameter

Equipment

1 pair of scissors

Knots used

Lark's head knot (see page 64)

Nested square knot (see page 64)

Alternating square knots (see page 67)

Open the hoop and stretch an 8 m length of 4 mm cord across the hoop one third of the way from the top, centring the cord. Wrap the cord on each side around the inner rim of the hoop, for around 65 tight turns, until the cords meet.

Close the hoop.

Tie 3 x 210 cm lengths of 4 mm cord onto the middle of the stretched cord using a lark's head knot, ensuring the lengths of cord are identical. Tie nested square knots until you reach the lower edge of the hoop. Open the hoop, wrap the end of the cords once around the inner hoop, keeping the cords taut, and then close the hoop.

On either side of the central strip of nested square knots, tie 12 x 240 cm lengths of 2 mm cable cord onto the stretched cord using lark's head knots.

On one side, tie 9 rows of alternating square knots spaced around 2.5 cm apart. Open the hoop, wrap the ends of the cords once around the inner hoop evenly and tautly, then close the hoop.

Repeat to make the other side. Tighten the screw of the hoop securely.

On one side of the central strip, separate the 24 ends of the cords into 4 groups of 6 cords. Tie 4 rows of alternating overhand knots of 6 cords each, decreasing by 1 knot per row to create a triangle and ending with 1 knot. Repeat on the other side.

Leave long, irregular fringes.

TECHNIQUES AND TIPS

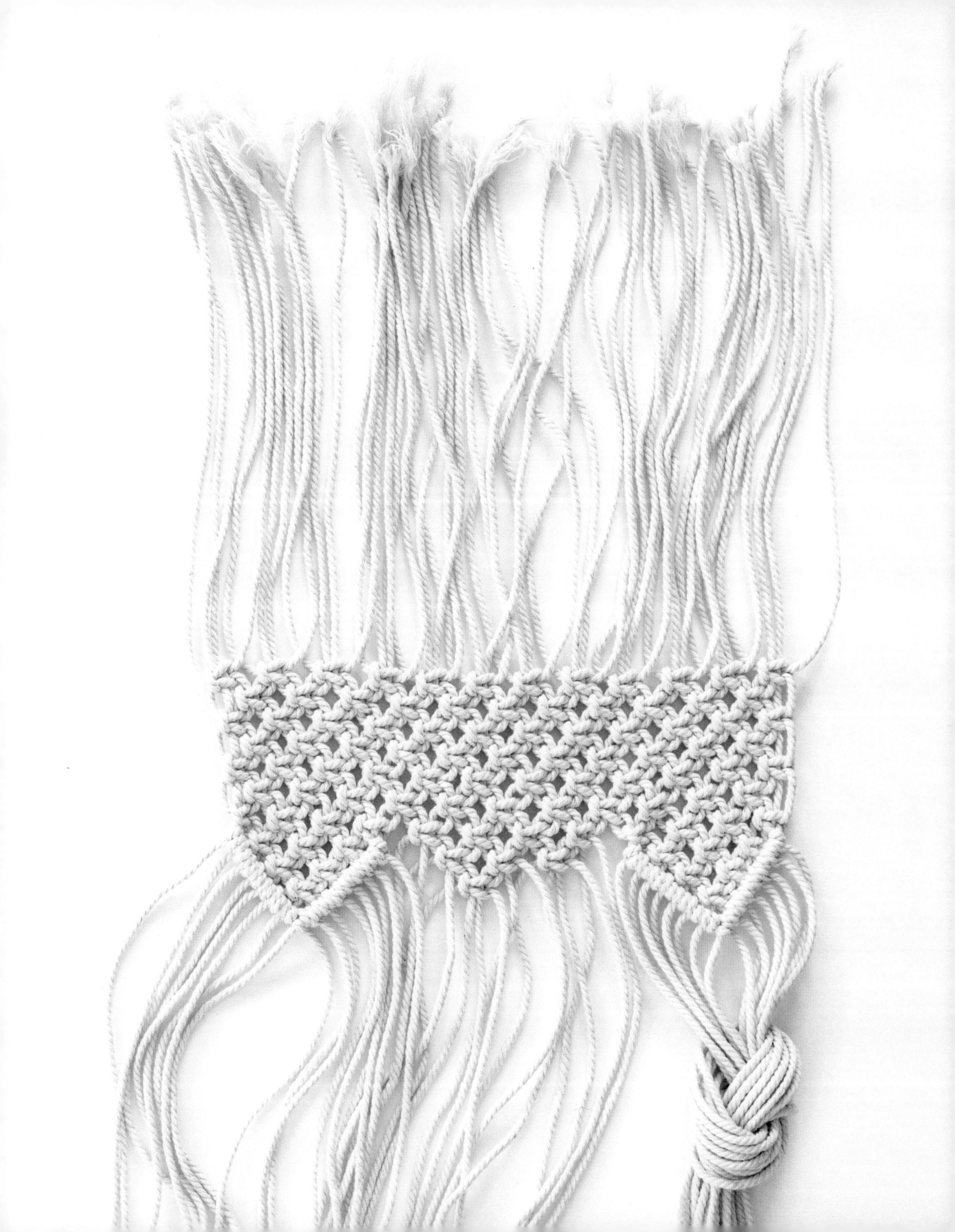

VEGETABLE DYE

This vegetable dyeing technique may not be orthodox (all the information on this subject can be found in specialist books) but it's extremely simple: have fun dyeing cord and textiles with ingredients you'll have in your kitchen to create decorative objects that won't need to be washed.

Whether you use carrot tops, onion peelings or avocado skin, the process is the same.

Recipe

You will need the tops from a bunch of carrots or a large handful of onion peelings or the skins of two avocados for a volume of 3 litres of water.

Boil the water, then add the carrot tops, onion peelings or avocado skins. Leave to boil for between 20 minutes and 1 hour depending on the colour you want to create. The longer you let it boil, the darker the result will be. Strain carefully. Place the cord in the dye bath you've created and heat it for 20 minutes to 1 hour. Drain the cord, wring out and leave to dry.

LARK'S HEAD KNOT

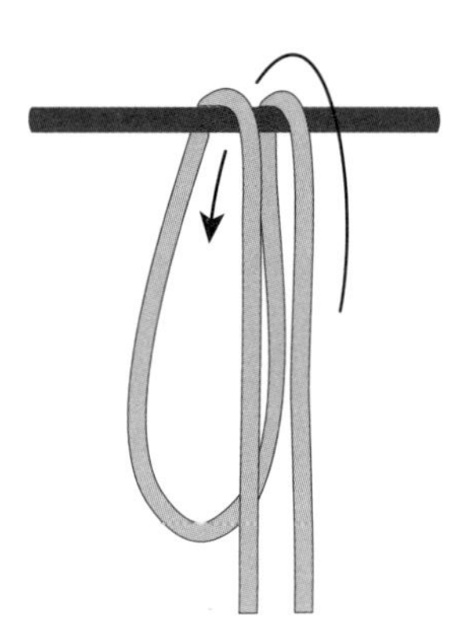

1. Fold the cord in half and place it over a dowel with the loop hanging down at the back.

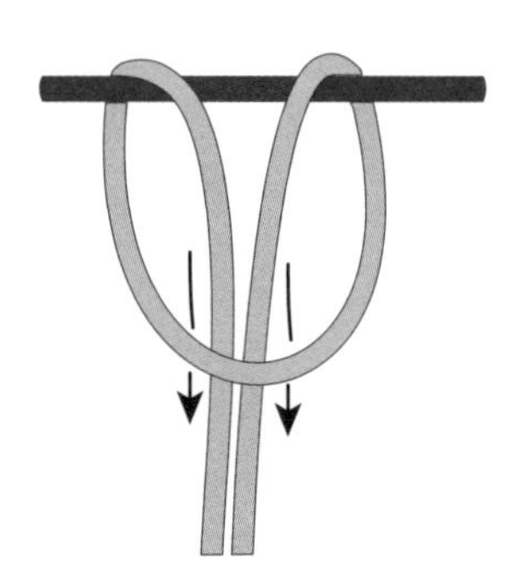

2. Pass the ends of the cord through the loop.

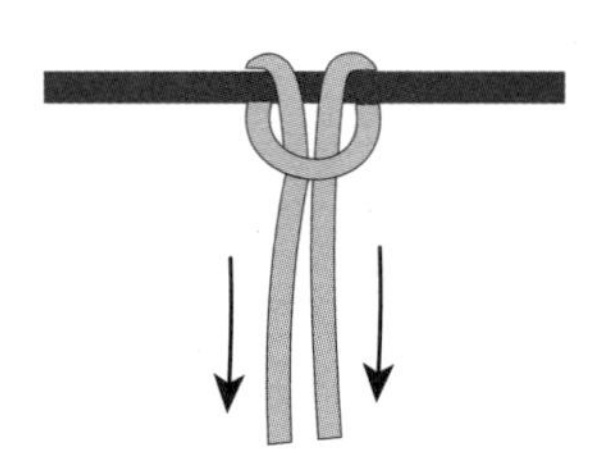

3. Tighten the cord onto the dowel, making sure that the two ends are the same length.

NESTED SQUARE KNOT

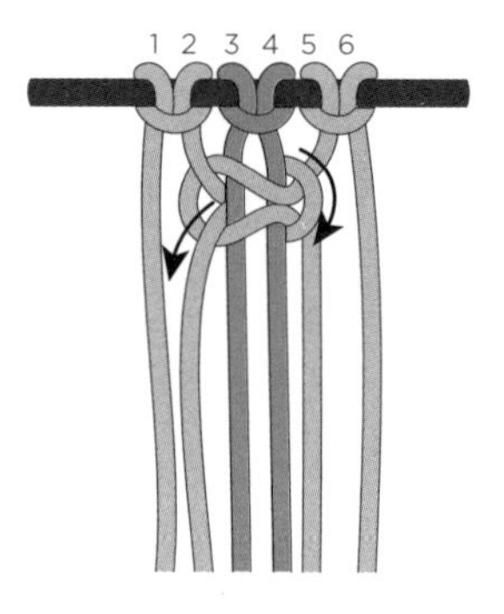

1. Tie a first square knot with cords 2 and 5 on the two filler cords 3 and 4.

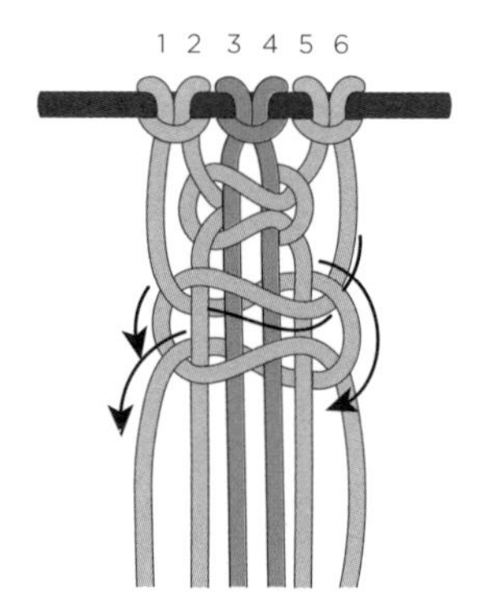

2. To tie the next square knot, use cords 1 and 6 on the 4 central cords.

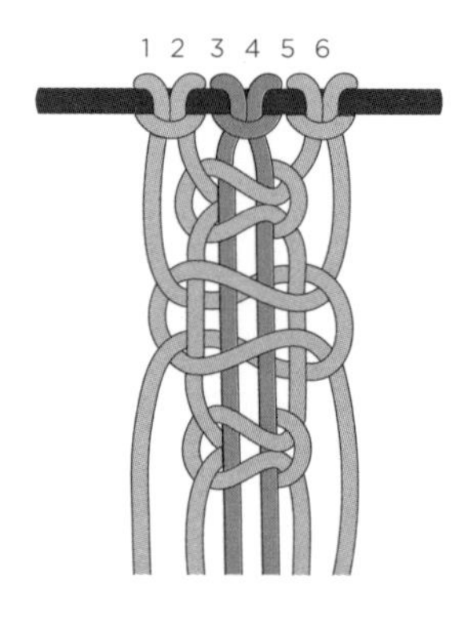

3. Alternate the square knots by repeating steps 1 and 2.

OVERHAND KNOT

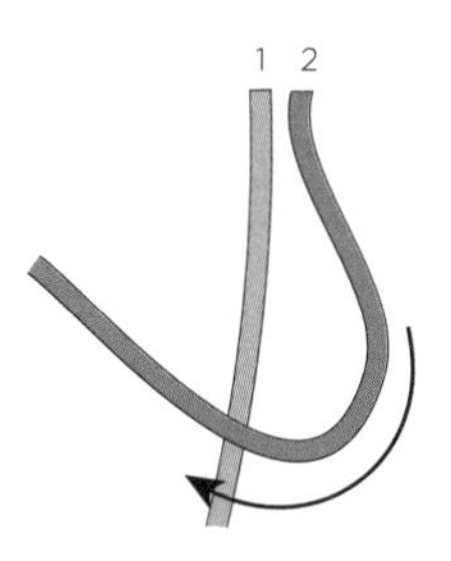

1. Pass right-hand cord 2 over left-hand cord 1.

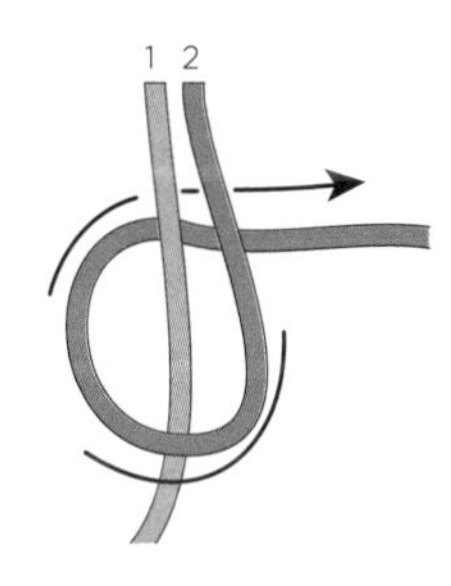

2. Bring cord 2 under cord 1 to form a loop.

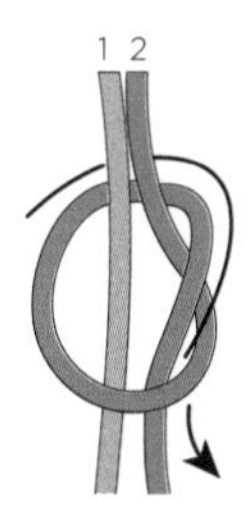

3. Pass cord 2 through the loop and tighten the knot.

DOUBLE OVERHAND KNOT

Tie a first overhand knot followed by a second and tighten it against the first knot.

REEF KNOT

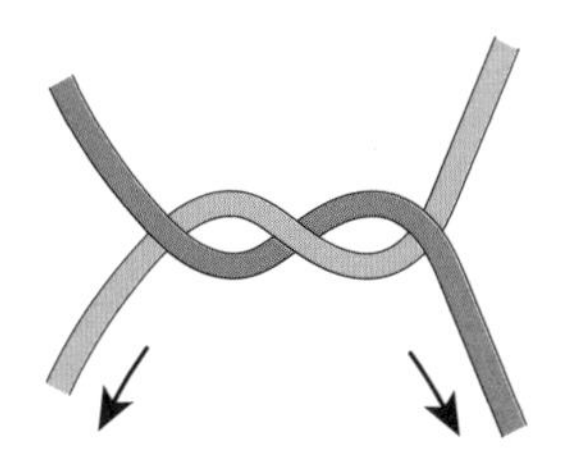

1. Cross the cords over each other twice.

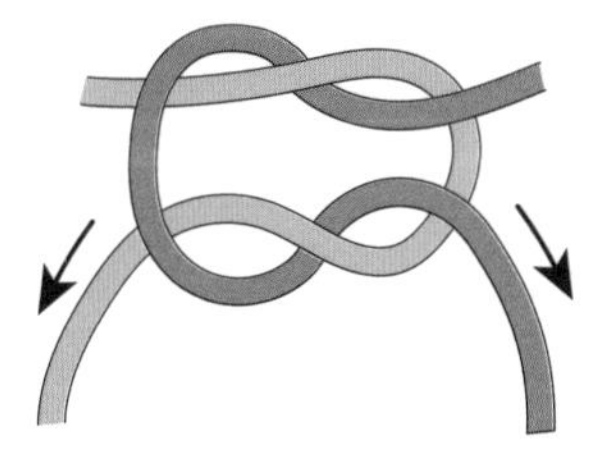

2. Make loops with the cords and cross them over.

3. Pull on the ends to form the knot and tighten.

SQUARE KNOT

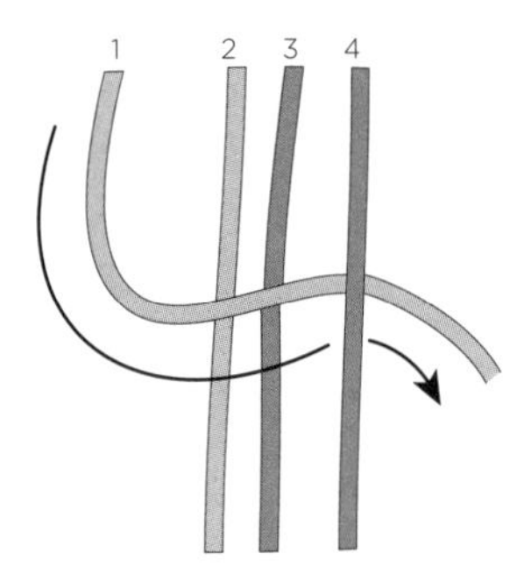

1. Half knot tied to the right: cross left-hand cord 1 over cords 2 and 3 and under right-hand cord 4.

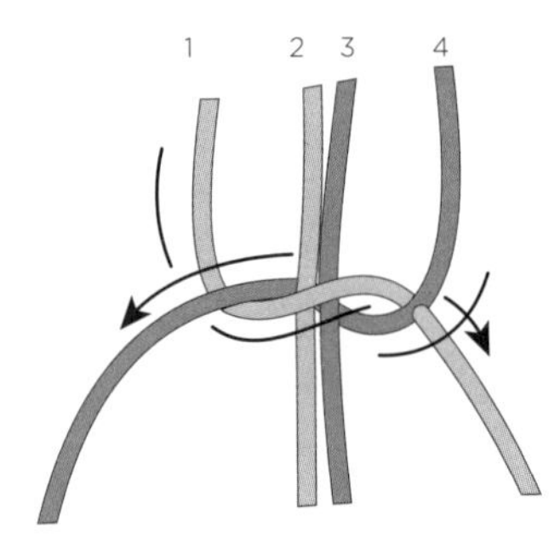

2. Pass right-hand cord 4 under cords 2 and 3 and over left-hand cord 1. This creates a half knot . Move it to the required height.

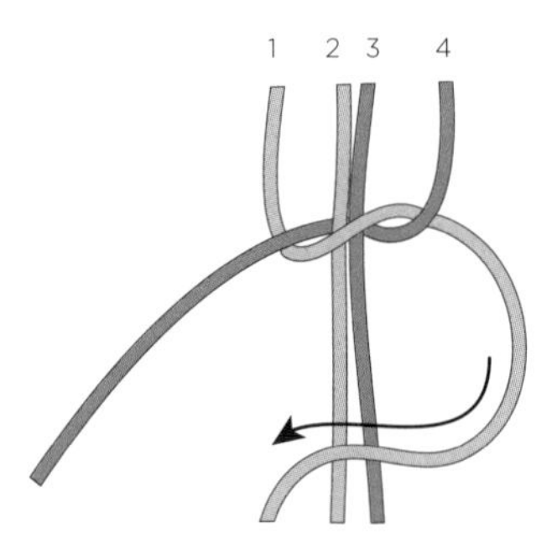

3. Half knot tied to the left: cross cord 1 over cords 3 and 2.

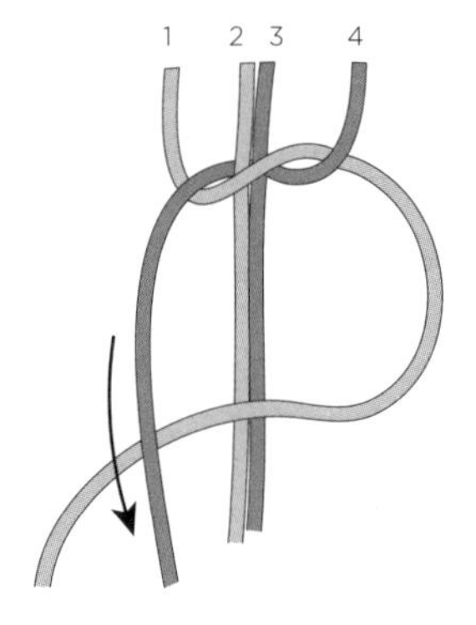

4. Pass cord 4 over cord 1.

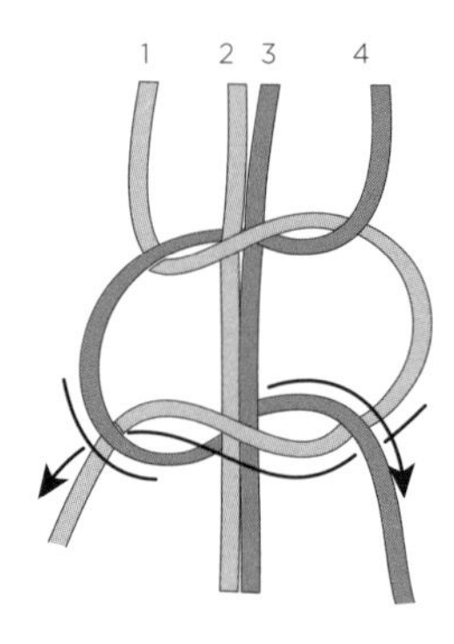

5. Pass cord 4 under cords 2 and 3 and over cord 1.

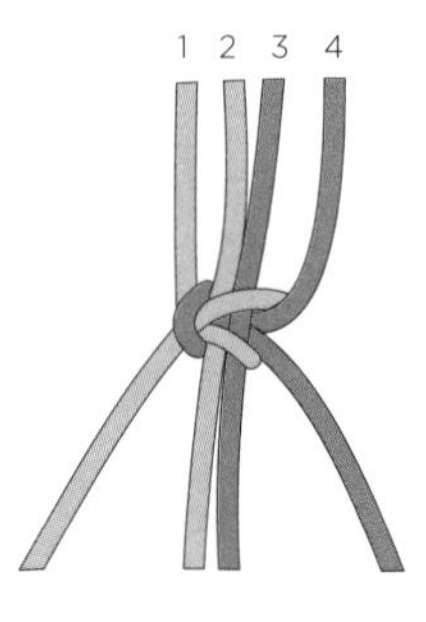

6. Tighten the square knot by pulling on cords 1 and 4.

HALF SQUARE KNOT SPIRAL

Continue to repeat steps 1 and 2 or steps 3 and 4. A succession of half-knots tied to the right or half knots tied to the left will naturally twist.

ALTERNATING SQUARE KNOTS

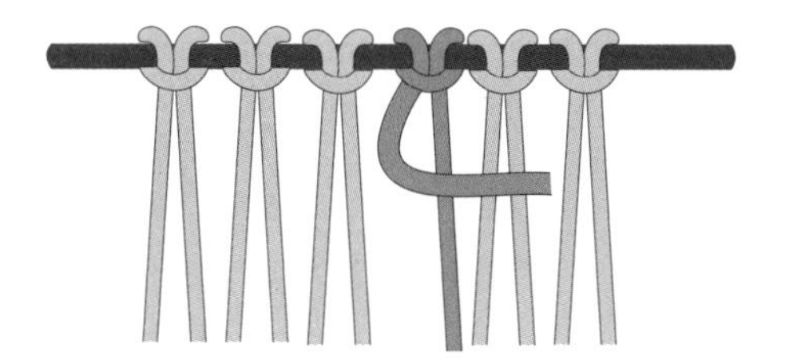

1. Alternating square knots are worked in groups of 4 cords.

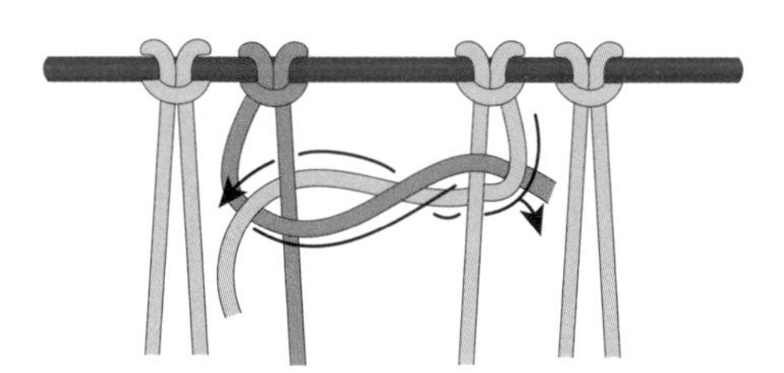

2. Create a half knot tied to the right on each group of 4 cords.

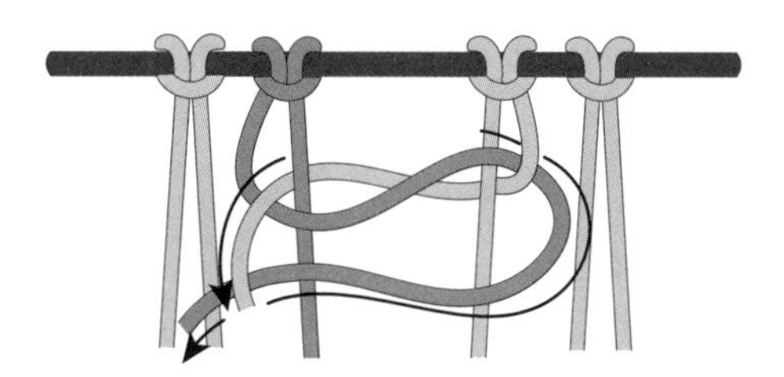

3. Complete the second half of the square knot on each group of 4 cords.

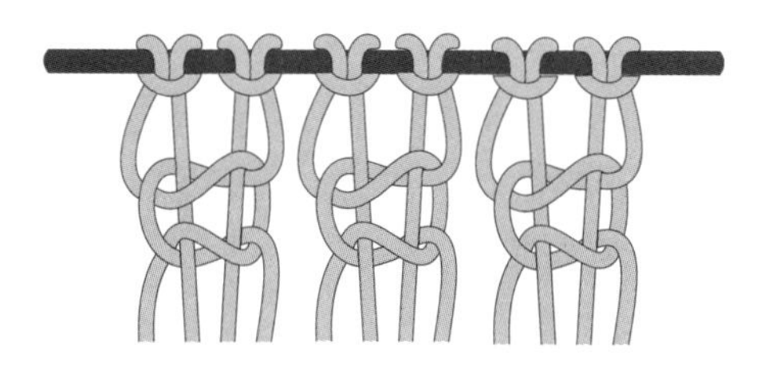

4. This creates a row of square knots side by side.

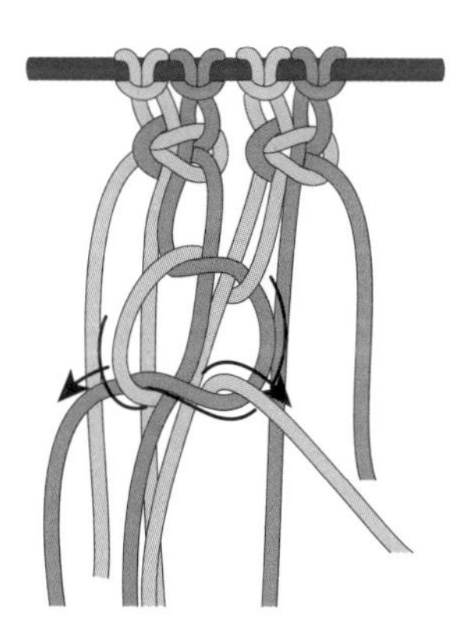

5. Tie the square knots on the second row by shifting the knots by two cords to the right to create a staggered pattern.

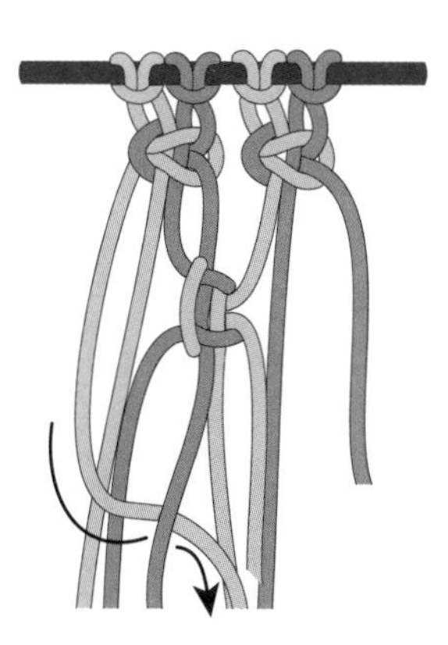

6. On the third row, tie the cords as in the first row. Keep repeating rows 1 and 2.

MONKEY'S FIST KNOT

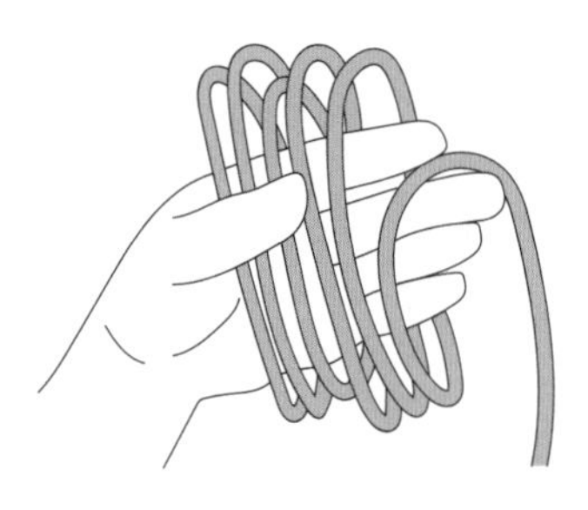

1. Wrap the cord vertically around the palm of one hand, and slide a small ball under the lines of cord. If it's easier, you can also hold the ball in your hand then wrap the cord around it.

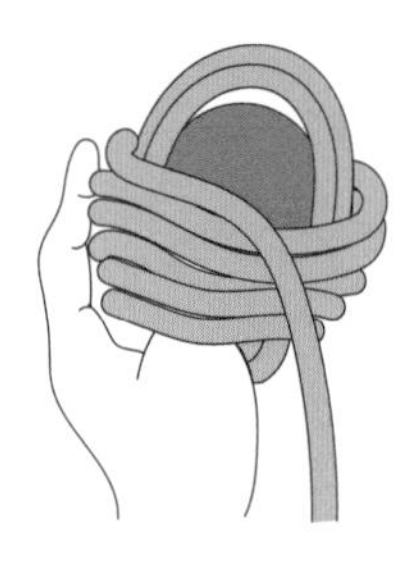

2. Then wrap the cord horizontally around the ball and the vertical lines of cord, pushing each line of cord tight against the other.

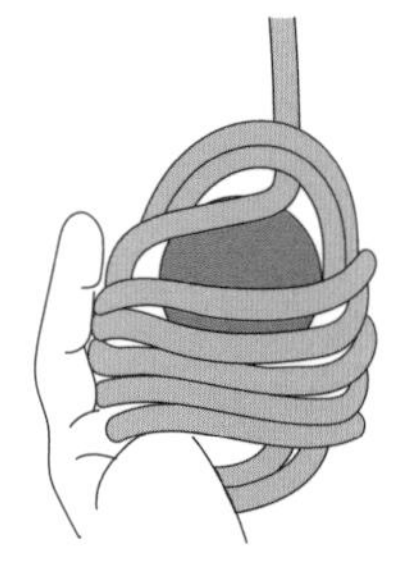

3. Thread the cord out at the top between the first vertical lines of cord and the ball.

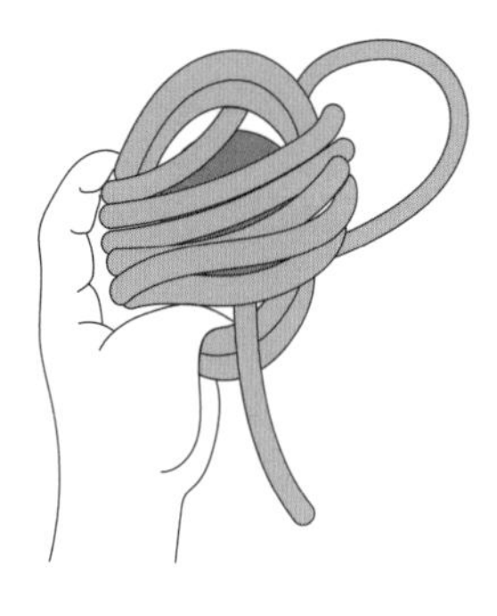

4. Thread the cord out at the bottom between the ball and the first vertical lines of cord.

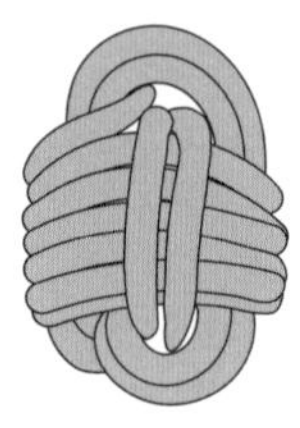

5. Continue to thread the cord up and down as in steps 3 and 4 until the ball is no longer visible.

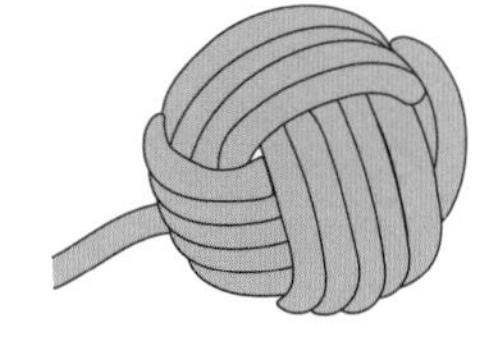

6. Starting with the first line of cord, pull on it to tighten each line of cord one after the other around the ball to create a tight monkey's fist knot.

ALTERNATING OVERHAND KNOT MESH

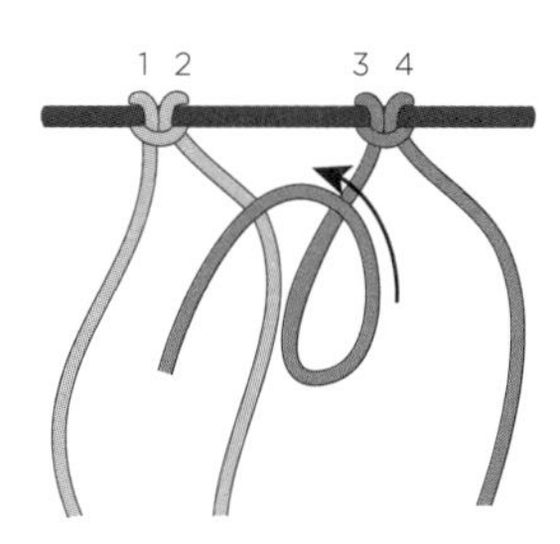

1. Start with 4 cords.
These cords will form the middle of the macrame mesh you are creating. Form a loop with cord 3.

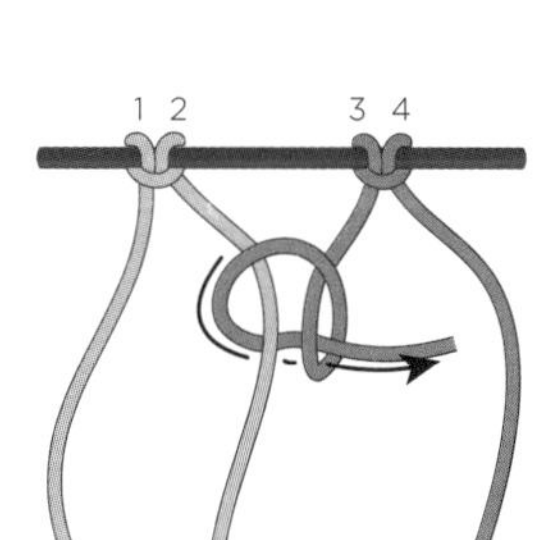

2. Pass the end of cord 3 under cord 2 and through the loop.

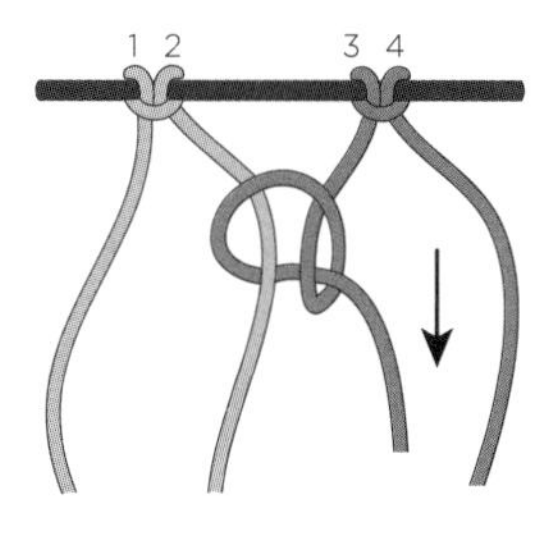

3. Tighten the knot on cord 2 by pulling cord 3 downwards.

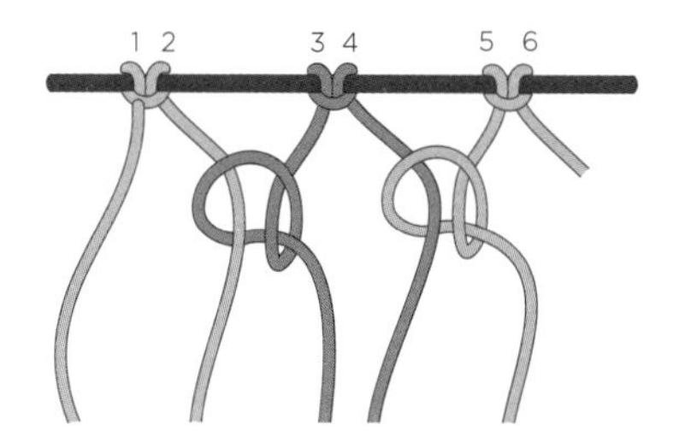

4. Work on both sides of this central knot. Form a knot with cord 5 around cord 4, at the same height as the previous knot, by repeating steps 1, 2 and 3.

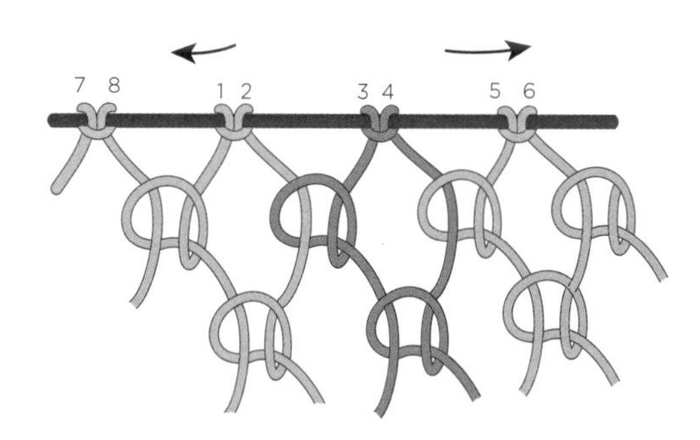

5. Form a knot with cord 1 around cord 8.

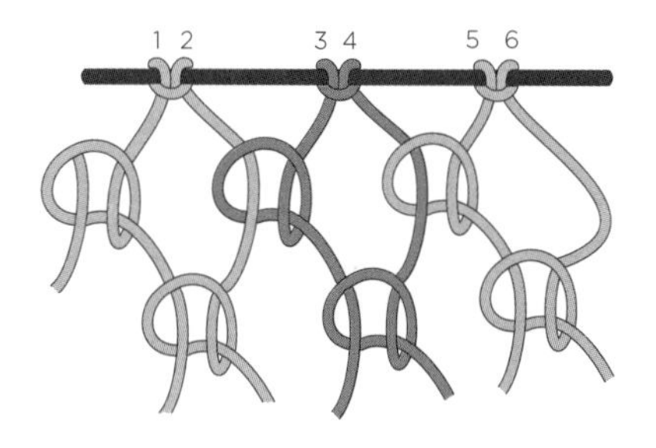

6. In the next row, the knots are tied to create a staggered pattern. Keep repeating these 2 rows.

HALF HITCH CHAIN

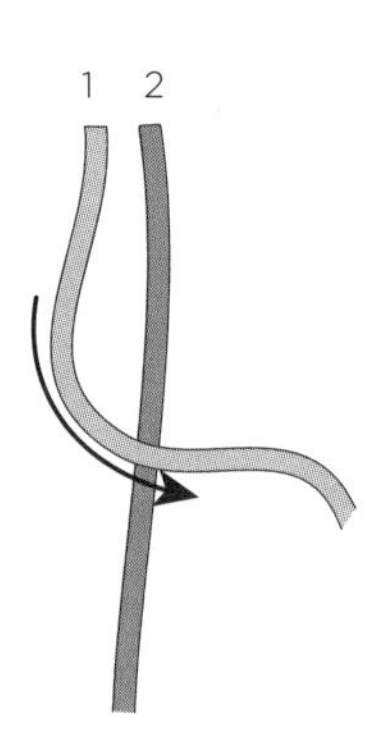

1. Form a loop by placing cord 1 over cord 2.

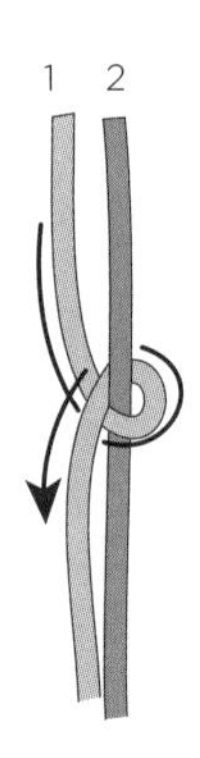

2. Pass cord 1 under cord 2 and thread it through the loop between cord 1 and cord 2.

3. Half hitch chains are always tied in the same direction.

GATHERING KNOT

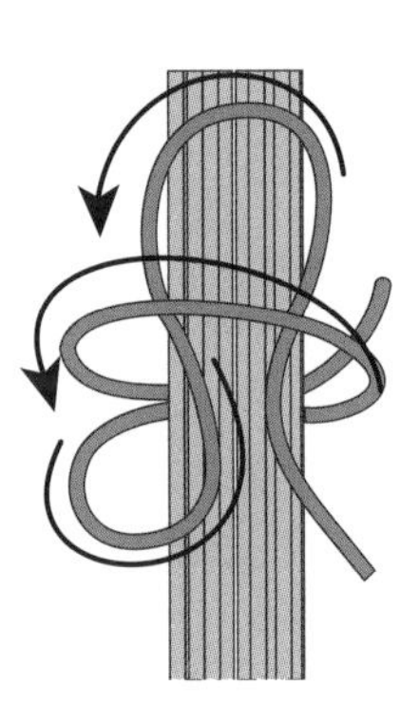

1. Gather the cords together. Form a loop over the cords with another piece of cord and wrap it around them, leaving one end free opposite the loop.

2. Continue wrapping this cord tightly around the

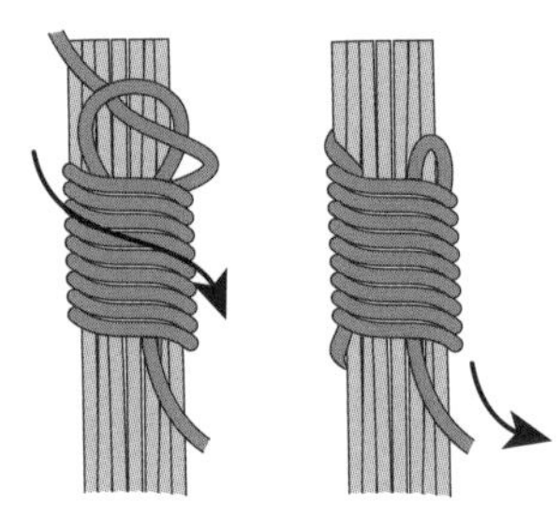

vertical cords, then pass the cord through the loop and pull. Use a needle to thread this end under the lines of cord then pull the end downwards.

JOSEPHINE KNOT

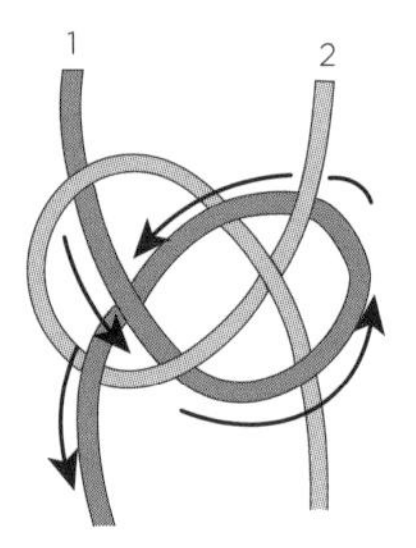

1. Make a loop with one cord. Thread a second cord through this loop to form a reverse loop.

MARINER'S BRAID

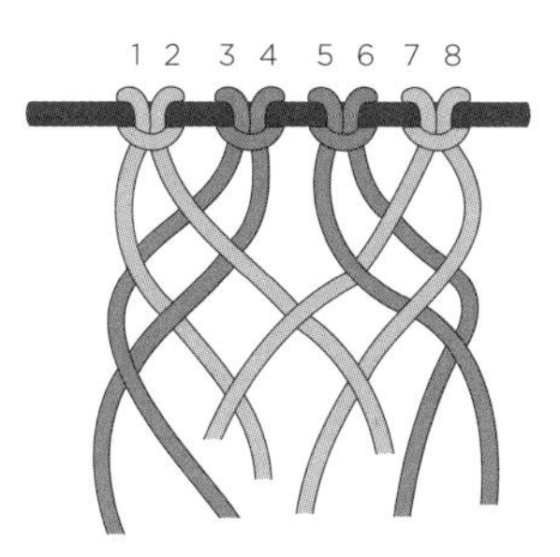

1. Work with 8 cords of the same length. Weave cords 1 and 2 and cords 7 and 8 as shown, directing them towards the inside of the braid.

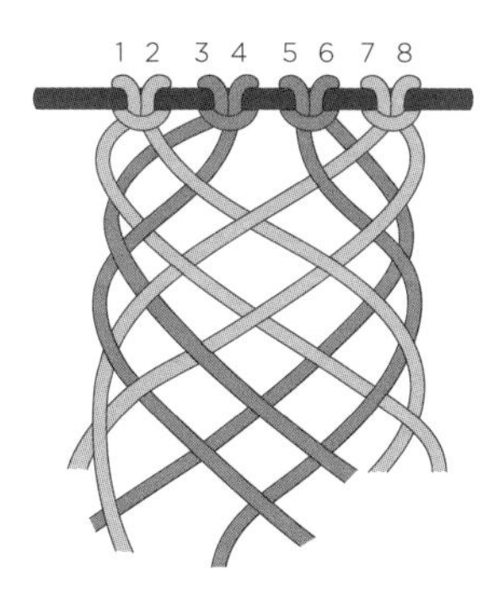

2. Weave cords 3 and 4 and 5 and 6, which are now on the outside, towards the inside of the braid.

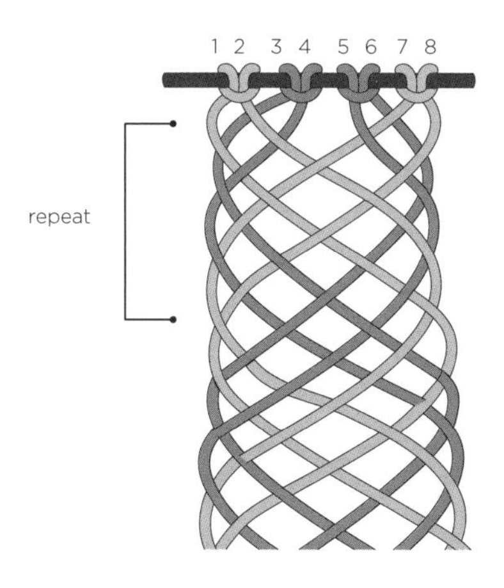

3. Keep weaving the 8 cords by repeating steps 1 and 2.

BOX KNOT BRAID

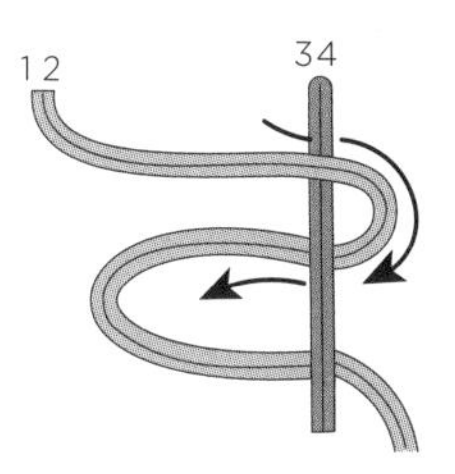

1. Work with 2 double cords. Form an S with cords 1 and 2. Position cords 3 and 4 vertically under the first loop of the S then over the next loop.

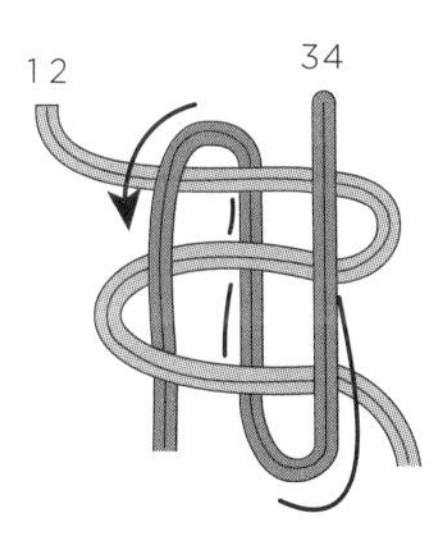

2. Fold cords 3 and 4 and thread them under the S. Fold them again then place them over the first loop of the S and under the last loop.

3. Form a loop with cord 1 and thread its end through the loop of cord 4. Pull the cords. Continue by repeating steps 5 and 6 with the other two cords in the opposite diagonal.

VERTICAL DOUBLE HALF HITCH

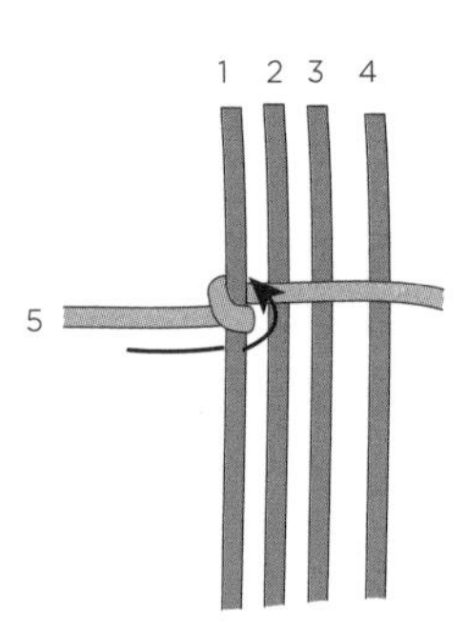

1. The vertical cords are filler cords.
Work with an additional cord 5, from left to right. Pass it under the first vertical cord 1 and wrap it around that cord to form a loop.

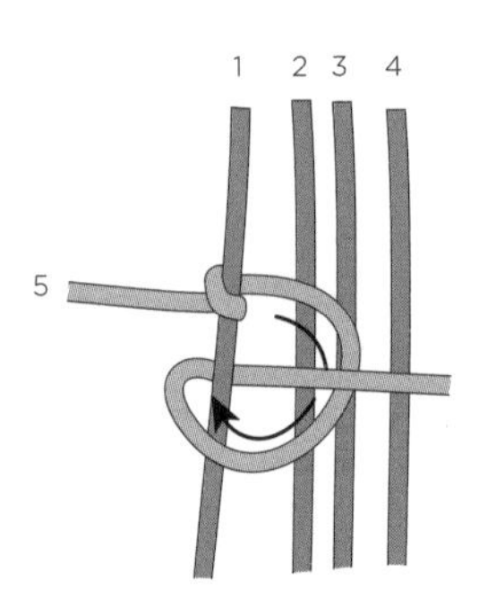

2. Bring cord 5 over cord 1, wrap it around cord 1 to form a loop and bring it out between the 2 loops.

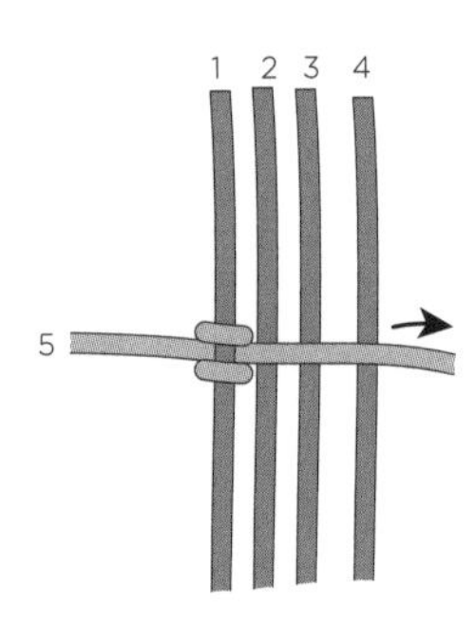

3. Gently tighten the knot formed by the two loops. Repeat steps 1 to 3 on cords 2, 3 and 4.

DIAGONAL DOUBLE HALF HITCH

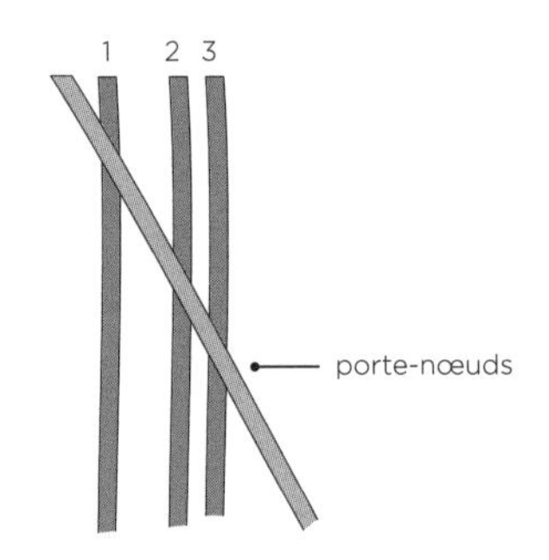

1. Position a cord diagonally on top of the other cords.

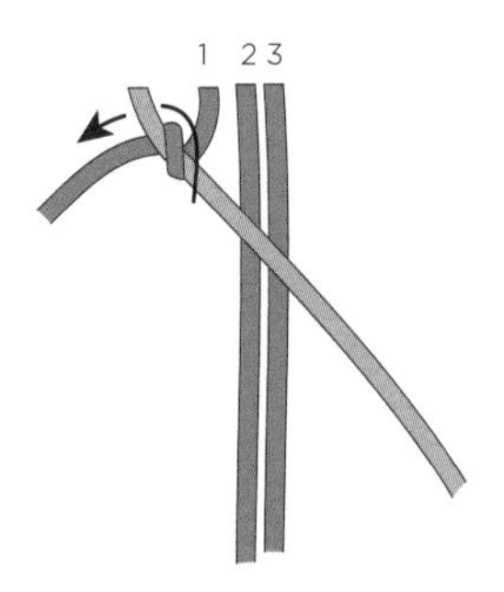

2. The first row is worked from left to right. Wrap cord 1 around the knot bearer to form a loop.

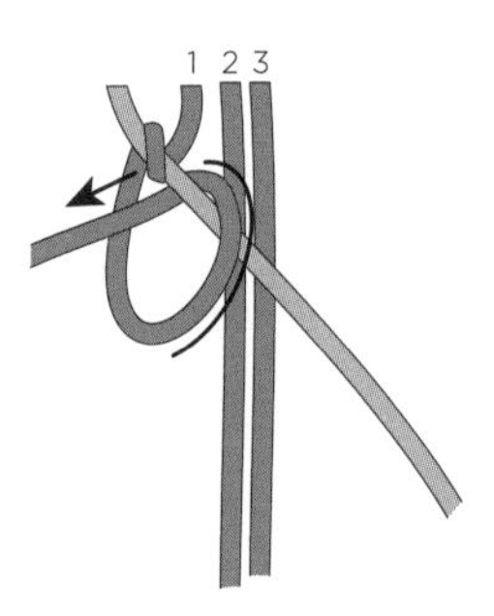

3. Wrap cord 1 around the knot bearer again to form a second loop and bring its end out between the two loops. Gently tighten the knot formed by the two loops. Repeat the same procedure with the other cords.

TWO ROWS OF VERTICAL

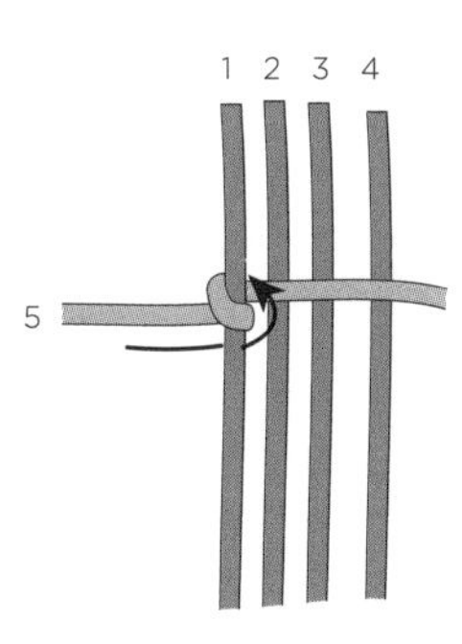

1. Arrange the cords vertically. Bring an additional cord 5 under the first vertical cord on the left and wrap it around it to form a loop.

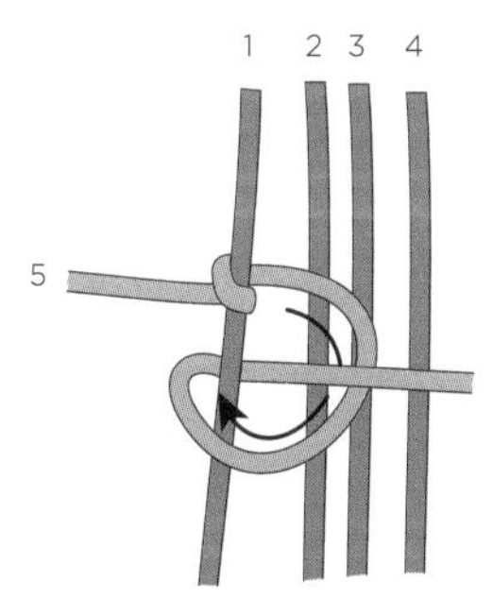

2. Bring cord 5 over cord 1, wrap it around it to form a loop and bring cord 5 out between the 2 loops.

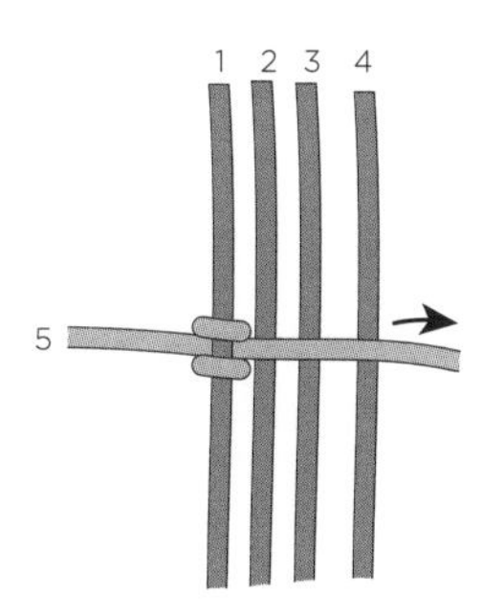

3. Gently tighten the knot formed by the two loops. Repeat steps 1 to 3 on cords 2, 3 and 4.

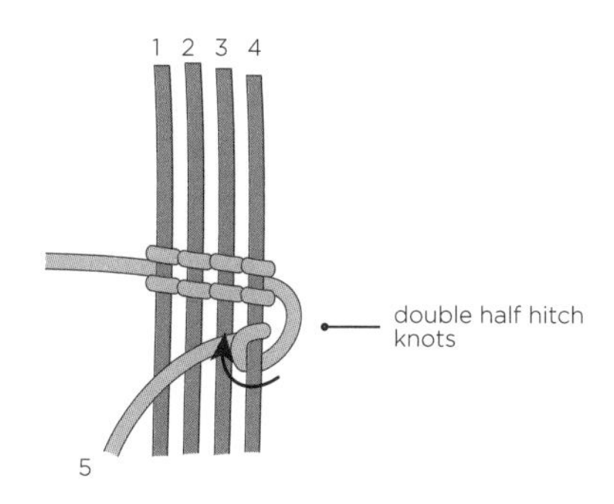

4. For the next row, bring cord 5 under cord 4 and wrap it around it to form a loop.

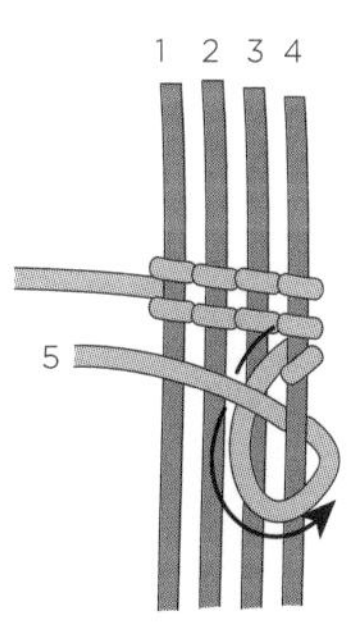

5. Bring cord 5 over cord 4 to form a loop and bring cord 5 out between the loops.

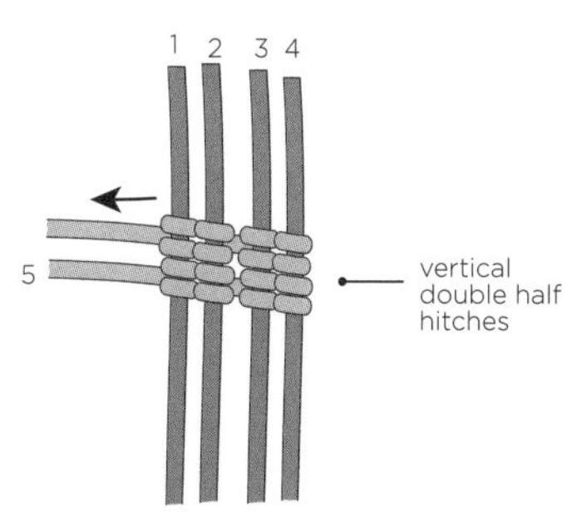

6. Repeat steps 4 and 5 across the whole row then tighten the rows together to create a vertical half hitch effect.

TWO ROWS OF DIAGONAL DOUBLE

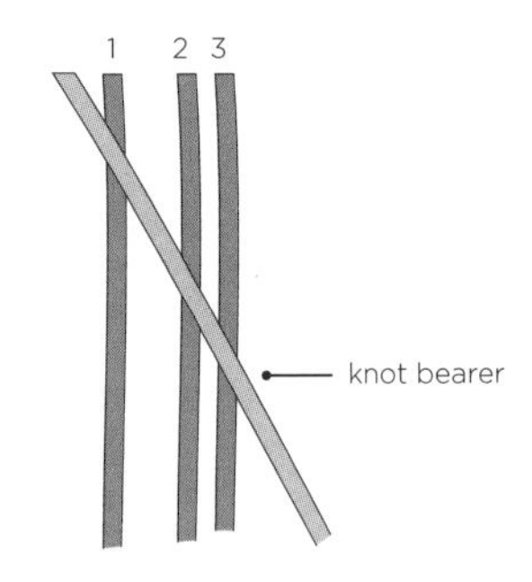

1. Position a cord diagonally on top of the other cords.

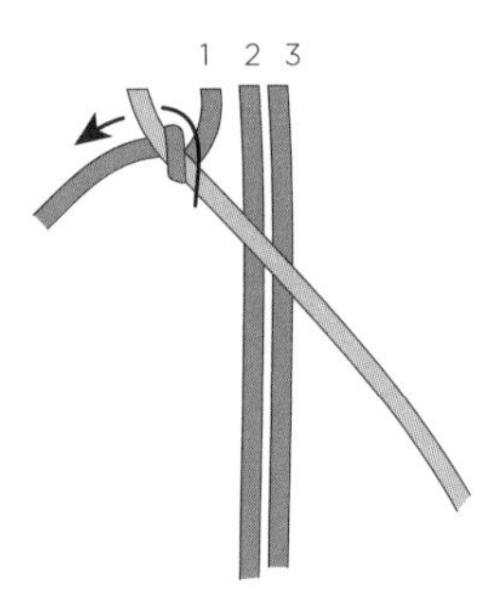

2. The first row is worked from left to right. Wrap cord 1 around the knot bearer to form a loop.

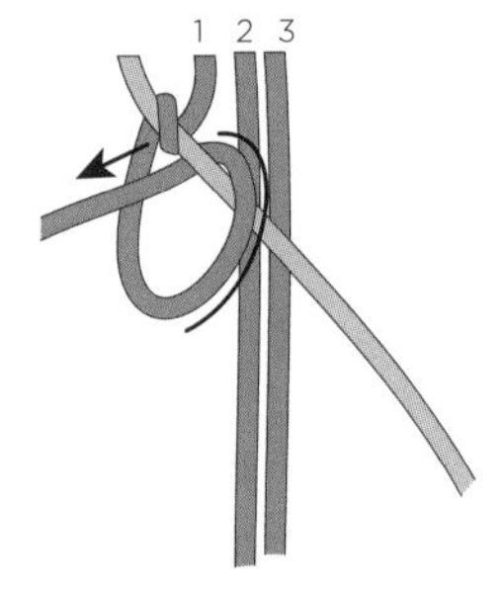

3. Wrap cord 1 around the knot bearer again to form a second loop and bring its end out between the two loops.

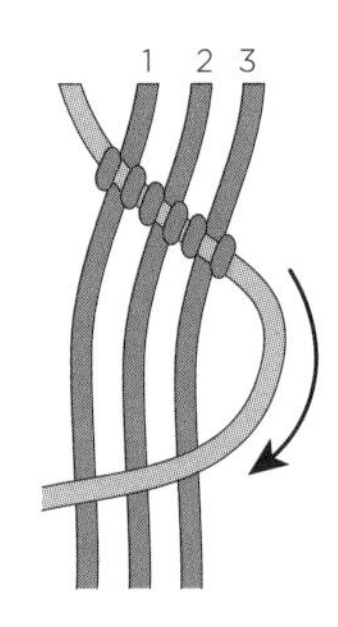

4. Gently tighten the knot formed by the two loops. Repeat steps 1 to 3 with cords 2 and 3.

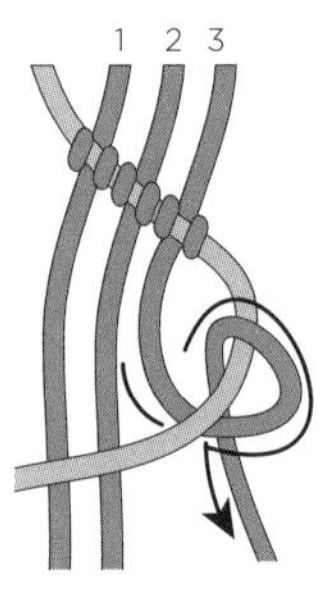

5. Work the second row from right to left. Fold the knot bearer diagonally in the opposite direction and wrap cord 3 around it to form a loop.

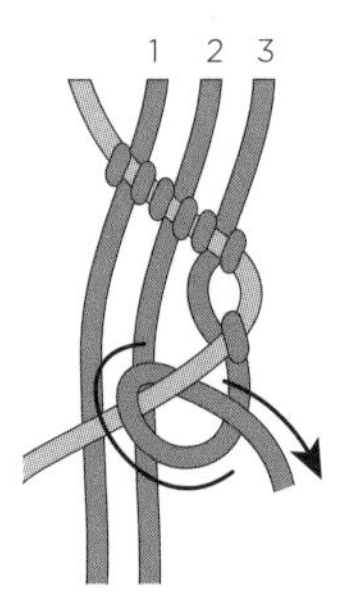

6. Make a second loop with cord 3 to form the first knot of the second row of diagonal double half hitches. Then tie cords 2 and 1 in the same way.

FRENCH KNITTING BOBBIN

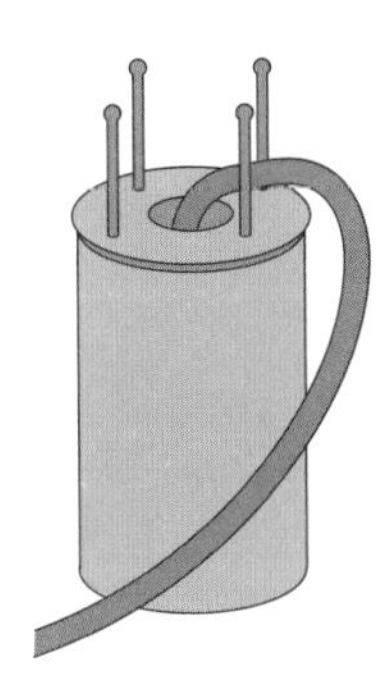

1. Thread the cord through the top of the knitting bobbin, leaving a tail end of around 15 cm at the bottom of the bobbin.

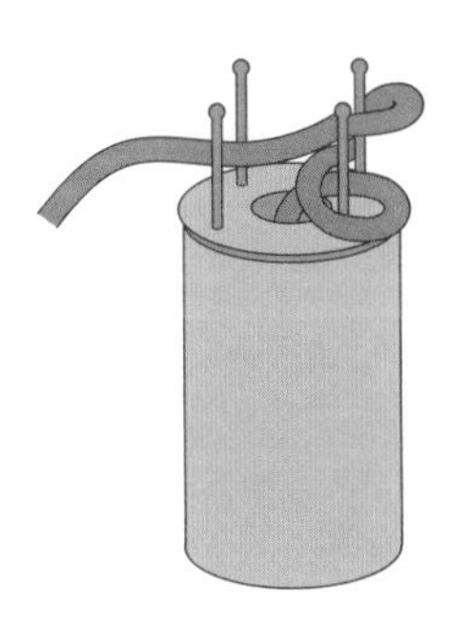

2. Keeping the tail end of the cord taut in the hand holding the bobbin, wrap the cord clockwise around one pin and then the next one.

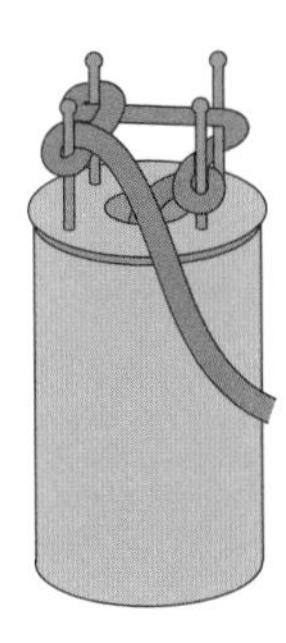

3. Wrap the cord around the other 2 pins in the same way, keeping the cord between the pins taut.

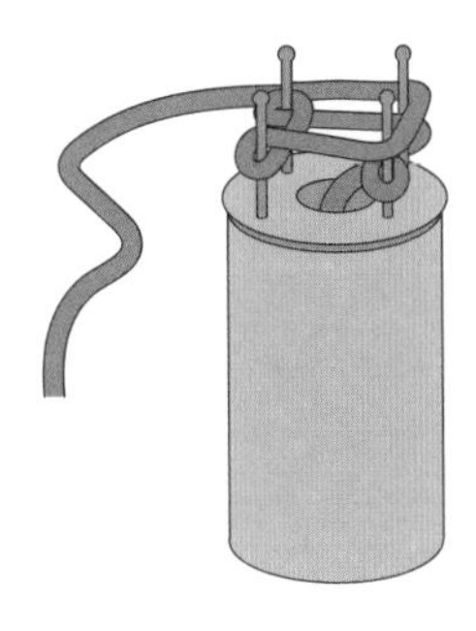

4. Now wrap the cord around the outside of the 4 pins and keep it taut.

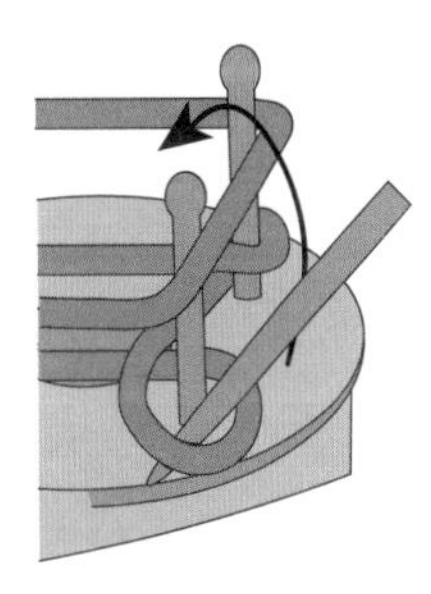

5. Use the tip of a knitting needle to pick up the lower cord wrapped around the first pin and pass it over the taut cord and over the pin. Repeat this procedure on the other 3 pins.

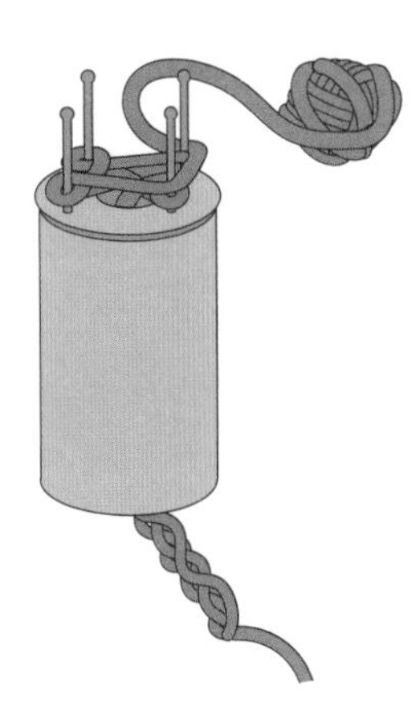

6. Then continue repeating steps 4 and 5. This will create a woven cord.

1. Depending on the size of cord chosen, to calculate the length of cord required for a project, generally allow 3 to 5 times the size of the finished project.
2. To avoid wasting cord, it's better to cut it as needed rather than cutting all the pieces at the start of a project.
3. Make sure you always fully tighten knots, as cotton cord tends to stretch over time.
4. Macramé can be created using a wide variety of materials: cotton cord of course, but also string, ribbons, wool, raffia, etc. Choose materials based on the nature of the project and what you have to hand.
5. Make sure you have enough cord to complete a project. It's better to have too much than not enough.
6. Prevent cord fraying by sticking a piece of masking tape or adhesive tape around the ends before starting a project.
7. Before starting a new project, practice tying the knots used on scrap pieces of cord in order to fully master them.
8. Use a white or ecru base cord to create varying shades of colour with vegetable dye.
9. Always apply the same tension to each cord and keep the spacing between knots regular.
10. Take time out from the stresses of everyday life to practice macramé. As you concentrate and focus your attention, this manual activity becomes a form of art therapy. Embrace its benefits and give your creativity free rein!

ACKNOWLEDGEMENTS

To Alexandra, my darling for ever and always, the first person to have seen my projects and given her feedback as they took shape. I hope you'll now want to try your hand at making one of them!

To Odile, Sylvie and Sophie, my loyal friends in the world of DIY (and so much more!).

To Pascale, who always knows what to say to stimulate creativity and good taste.

To Julie, for her lovely photos that showcase my designs so perfectly.

To Lucie, for her pencil lines and drawings – essential for understanding the knots and doing it so much better than words ever could!

To my family and the latest new arrival, Alexandre.

To Sébastien, for his beautiful and delicious pretzels that have inspired much of my macramé (at the end of the day, it always comes down to this: good food and DIY go hand in hand and are inseparable!).

To my gourmet friends Isabelle and Nicolas Bernardé, the amazing team from La Garenne.

To Christophe Felder and all his wonderful cake recipes that have kept me going through the long hours of designing and making my projects, and to Serge Knapp, always there even at a distance.

This edition published in 2024 by Hardie Grant Books, an imprint of Hardie Grant Publishing.

Hardie Grant Books (London)
5th & 6th Floors
52–54 Southwark Street
London SE1 1UN

British Library Cataloguing-in-Publication Data. A catalogue record for this book is available from the British Library.

Macramé
ISBN: 9781784887599
10 9 8 7 6 5 4 3 2 1

58, rue Jean-Bleuzen - 92178 Vanves Cedex
978-2-501-15707-0

Designer: Frédéric Voisin
Illustrator: Lucy Téxier
Proofreading: Dominique Montembault

Publishing Director: Kajal Mistry
Typesetting: David Meikle
Translation: Alison Murray
Proofreader: Lindsay Kaubi
Production controller: Gary Hayes
Colour reproduction by p2d
Printed and bound in China by RR Donnelley Paper Products Ltd.